Wine Faults

Causes, Effects, Cures

Wine Faults
Causes, Effects, Cures

John Hudelson, Ph.D.
Foreword by John Buechsenstein

The Wine Appreciation Guild
San Francisco

The Wine Appreciation Guild
360 Swift Avenue
South San Francisco, CA 94080
(650) 866-3020
www.wineappreciation.com

Library of Congress Cataloging-in-Publication Data
Hudelson, John.
  Causes, effects, cures / John Hudelson.
    p. cm.
  Includes bibliographical references and index.
  ISBN 978–1–934259–63–4
  1. Wine and wine making—Analysis. 2. Wine and wine making—Chemistry. 3. Wine blending. 4. Wine—Color. I. Title.
  TP548.5.A5H83 2010
  641.2'20287—dc22   2010043658
        Editor: John Buechsenstein.
        Consulting Editor: Anna Katharine Mansfield, Ph.D.

Citations:
Graph, of Rapp Nahrung 1998 on pages 10 and 11 © Copyright 2010 by and used with the permission of Gavin Sacks,
Asst. Professor of Enology, Dept. of Food Science and Technology, NYS Agricultural Experiment Station, Cornell University,
Geneva, N.Y. 14456.

Printed in the United States of America
10 9 8 7 6 5 4 3 2 1

Table of Contents

Foreword

We who are frequent tasters are constantly on the prowl for wines of quality. When asked for a definition, a professor once told our class: "Quality is the absence of faults." Never satisfied with an apparently glib reply we proceeded to debate this rather simplistic definition, particularly since we'd heard that many great wines possessed at least some defects. We were then lectured that these defects are often present at sub-threshold levels, begging analogy to the proverbial tree falling in the woods with nobody there to hear it.

Our questions continued: How were we to recognize these faults when their increasing concentration brought them up to detectable levels? Were they not reputed, in some cases, to increase complexity and, in some regions contribute to a localized collection of flavor idiosyncrasies known as *terroir*? When did they constitute faults?

This is the no-man's-land of perception, somewhere between sub- and supra-threshold, where faults begin to be detected, grow to be recognized, and can eventually dominate a wine's aromatics. Professor Hudelson enables us to "know our enological enemies" and that knowledge, combined with tasting experience, will help us differentiate faults from attributes, understand their origins and prevention, and put them in perspective. In an accessible and practical narrative he reminds us frequently that "the dose makes the poison," echoing the sentiment of experienced tasters who realize that faults at lower levels may be attributes that add to complexity but at higher levels, render the wine defective.

In another instance a celebrity vintner lectured us on his laissez-faire winemaking philosophy and, with obviously false modesty, maintained that his best wines were the product of his "benign neglect." I learned during my first few weeks as a working enologist that neglect, benign or otherwise, was a recipe for disaster. Wine is a natural product, always susceptible to change. Even when less manipulation is better, vigilance is of utmost importance!

Wine tasters, whether they are students, teachers, winemakers, sommeliers or consumers, need to be able to recognize and evaluate faults in wine. Much as we'd like to believe that in this modern era with all our knowledge and technology we needn't worry, they will always be with us, lurking behind complacency and ignorance, ready to bite us in the rear if we ignore them.

My wish list during many years as a wine teacher has included a ready reference for wine defects. So often researching any one flavor problem involved sifting through indexes, pulling several textbooks off the shelf, and finding an explanation requiring instant recall of long-forgotten biochemistry. Then came the problem of translating this information to convey it to students.

Problem solved! This book is written in the voice of a teacher who understands the type of organized presentation and friendly delivery that will succeed with students. It is comprehensive, going beyond the "usual suspects" (corked, VA, Brett) and even reviewing some taints that are quite rare. There is enough depth and detail to be immensely useful to wine instructors and pupils while avoiding an overload of minutiae. It is obviously the product of a rich career that has accumulated wisdom through hands-on laboratory and sensory detective work.

As a long time teacher of wine sensory evaluation, I applaud the collection of so much information into a sensible, accessible monograph. If you're in any way connected to wine, read this book and don't let it get far from reach.

Thank you, Professor!

John Buechsenstein
Wine Educator
University of California Davis Extension
Culinary Institute of America, Greystone

Preface

Wine Faults may not be the most propitious title for this manual. Nobody likes faults or being at fault or, especially, having caused a fault. This book is designed to help winemakers avoid, evaluate and correct wine faults. But it is not just for winemakers. You may have picked up this book because you are an oenophile, wine blogger, wine judge or just a wine fanatic trying to better understand those off-flavors you have too often tasted. In that case, this manual is also for you. I have attempted to stay away from the enological jargon and have simplified the chemistry. A glossary at the back of the book will help explain specialized terms.

I came to the writing of this book after 35 years of winemaking. Most of the hundreds of wines that I made had flaws. As the old proverb declares, "By ignorance we mistake, and by mistakes we learn." After many wine chemistry courses through Cornell University's Cooperative Extension, and during years of working as a wine chemist in a large kosher winery, I learned to make good, stable wines with no obvious faults. But most of my education on faults is a result of being open to the evaluation of others. Unless you are outstandingly lucky—or your name is Bacchus—openness is essential to producing good wine. Too often a winemaker avoids outside evaluation. As a result, a flawed "house palate" develops over time. Every winemaker needs triangulation through trials, candid appraisals and competitions. So, the most important precept for learning about wine faults is this: leave your ego at the door.

The manual is divided into four sections. The first covers the processes by which we detect flaws and faults in wine: visual, olfactory, taste, and mouth feel. This section also covers the constituents of wine and how they change through time and hide or emphasize faults. The second section looks at faults that emanate from the vineyard as well as non-biotic contamination. The canon that good wine is made in the vineyard is only half the story; bad wine can be made in the vineyard too. Choices such as when to harvest will affect alcohol and acid levels. More than ever today in warm climates—and possibly exacerbated by global warming—those choices may result in very unbalanced high alcohol wines with low natural acids. These wines become perfect precursors for biotic infections. Wine is a living organism. It is filled with living organisms and chemicals that change with time. The third section is a compendium of just what can go wrong when the winemaker does not guard against simple unwanted organisms. Throughout the book, when possible, I have suggested precautions and solutions. I have also offered a typology key that may help the novice determine which wine fault he or she is sensing.

I have many people to thank for starting me on this book, encouraging me and assisting on the way to the final draft. It is not my work alone, but I take responsibility for any mistakes that it may contain. I give homage to chemists large and small who affected the way I see the world, including Michael Reeske, who taught me that "the dose makes the poison"; Michael Migliore, the consummate winemaker, Robert Constantino of Santé and Paul O'Herron, *valde explecater*. I am appreciative of Eli and Michael Herzog's support in my education on large-scale wine chemistry. I thank those from academia:

Thomas Hennic-Kling, Charles Edwards and Jim Harbertson of Washington State University; Gavin Sacks, Alan Lasko, and Anna K Mansfield at Cornell University; Andrew Waterhouse of University of California Davis and Bruce Zoecklein of Virginia Tech. The inspiration for this manual was a Wine Faults course that I teach at Central Washington University, and I would like to thank the people who supported this course, Kevin Nemeth and Dr. Jan Bowers. Finally, I owe so much of my success (but none of my faults) to Carol Pauli, editor, counselor and wife extraordinaire.

How We Sense
(or fail to sense)
Wine Faults

We use most of our senses when we taste wine (although only sparkling wine should make a sound). The protocol for judging the quality of a wine starts with its appearance, followed by its smell. After that, in the mouth both taste and odor along with what judges call "mouth feel" (related to touch) affect our perception of the wine. This chapter examines how our senses work to interpret what we are tasting, and suggests what constitutes acceptable limits for unflawed wine. It also describes the basic components of wine, what differentiates a flaw from a fault, and ends with a taxonomic key for identifying and defining them.

Defining Flaws and Faults

Wines will often have bouquets and flavors that are atypical for the variety of that wine. This is usually considered a flaw by judges, lowering the wine's score, even when bouquet or flavor is not necessarily objectionable. A flowery Chardonnay with herbal notes more associated with Gewürztraminer might be an example of a "pleasantly flawed" wine. A light-bodied Nebiolo from Borolo with violet notes might be another. But what about a rosé the bright pink of Pepto Bismol? The assumption of what a flaw is will vary by region and intensity (see page 56, "Is there a Petroleum Crisis…in Riesling").

Most flaws are associated with unpleasant tastes and smells. A wine flaw is experienced as a minor departure from what is usually characteristic of that variety, appellation and style. One flaw should not make a wine undrinkable or eliminate it from a competition.

The difference between a flaw and a fault is a question of degree: when the flaw becomes so disagreeable that it makes the wine undrinkable or renders its bouquet repulsive, it has become a fault. An example of this is the molecule *4-ethyl-phenol* associated with Brettanomyces, which in small amounts can add complexity to red wine, with odors described as "horsey" or "sweaty-saddles," but in greater concentration becomes a fault that smells like "band aids." Unfortunately, our reactions to some atypical smells and flavors are so strong that they can only be faults. Tyrene (T.C.A. or "corkiness") is one such smell, which can be detected at *3 parts-per-trillion* (ng/L) and almost always ruins a wine. An exception to this "degree of atypical bouquet and taste" rule is chemical contamination. It is not always detectable by our senses but is always a fault even when not above the legal limit.

The point at which a flaw becomes a fault is somewhat arbitrary. People differ as to their sensitivity and acceptance of a flaw. Some people have tried to quantify the point at which flaws become faults. Although the following table, resulting from numerous wine competitions of the British Columbia Amateur Wine Makers Association, does not attempt to do such, it does list the ratio (in percentage) of flaws to faults for each problem and the degree to which the fault is the responsibility of the winemaker (PW).

Name of Problem	Flaw	Fault	PW
Brettanomyces Contamination	80%	20%	0
Tyrene (T.C.A.= corkiness)	20%	80%	0
Chemical Contaminants	0	100%	100%

Flaws of Appearance

While the quality of appearance weighs in low behind odor and taste, it is often a harbinger of what is to come in a wine. The American Wine Society counts appearance for only 15% of its score, but descriptively, visual cues tell the taster much about the condition of the wine. If the wine tastes as if it is "old," is losing its fruit, has become maderized, or is very soft, the taster will often look at the color again for supporting evidence that the wine may be past its age. Or if off-odors are dominant, the taster may correlate these with a lack of clarity in the wine. The following are just a few of the aspects of appearance that should be considered when looking for faults in wine.

Color

Every variety and blend of wine has a particular range of colors associated with it. The components of the colors, anthocyanins for red wines and flavonols for whites, will vary the color of the wine over time by chemical interactions—anthocyanins with tannins and catechins, flavonols with oxygen. The pH of the wine will also affect the color, hue, saturation, chroma and intensity as is seen in the delphinidin-3-glucoside coloring in water to the right (one hue, three colors). The overall color in a red wine will move from bright red toward purple as the pH increases.

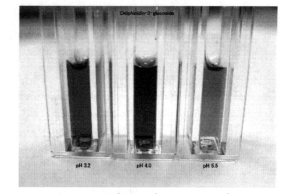

www.arakoonwines.com.au/

Generally, the higher the pH in a white wine, the greater the tendency of the wine to be toward the amber end of the spectrum. Low pH, high acid wines tend to be toward the lighter pale straw end of the spectrum (but this does not hold for fortified wines such as Sherry or late harvest wines where the sugars can affect color change).

Variations in the color of a wine may be directly related to the wine's soundness, age and longevity. When the color of a wine is skewed to one end of the hue or to a very low or high color saturation it suggests other flaws soon to be discovered. But can we say a wine has a color fault? If a white (or red) wine is brown, then yes, and it is likely the first of many faults for that wine. Also, there are no naturally occurring dark green wines, bright blue or Pepto Bismol pink wines. Such colors can only mean adulteration, and therefore such wines have faults.

Clarity

Whereas an off-color will never be the *only* fault of a wine, the clarity—translucence, lack of insoluble particles—can be. Since the beginning of the micro-brew-beer era, several wineries have been adamant about not fining or filtering their wines. Non-fined or filtered wines—especially those produced by large corporations like Mondavi—can be

sound. But maintaining soundness requires laboratory work and quality control. Many small wineries that try to emulate such production end up with wines that remain cloudy long after bottling.

High pH will decrease the charge on suspended particles allowing them to stay suspended in solution longer. (Likewise, the use of gelatin and other positively charged ions to remove tannins, yeast and bacteria in wine of high pH will make the wine even more cloudy.) Chilling can bring on hazes or casse in wines not properly cold or heat stabilized. And finally, judges often suspect the worst when they see cloudy wine; the worst in this case is a bacterial infection causing ropiness, or sediment caused by the yeast *Zygosaccharomyces bailii* (see page 52).

André Karwath, Wikimedia

Carbonation

Even in sparkling wine, the atypical size and activity of the bubbles can be a flaw. In still wine, bubbles are absolutely a fault (although sometimes a pleasant one) which suggests incomplete fermentation, post bottling malolatic fermentation or some unwanted lactic acid bacteria (LAB) such as *Pediococcus spp* (see page 50).

Mouth Feel

"*Mouth feel*" is the feel and weight of a wine in the mouth. Two faults associated with appearance can be best experienced by mouth feel: carbonation and viscosity. The least little prickle of bubbles can be sensed on the tongue through mechano-receptors. Likewise the "heaviness" of a wine is also perceived that way. A heavy wine can be the result of sugar, in which case it may be judged normal. A "thick" wine may also be the result of glycerol, a higher alcohol that gives body to the wine.

The heat generated by high alcohol is generally sensed by thermo-afferent receptors and can be negative. The "legs" that form above the wine in a balloon glass are really just alcohols condensing and running down the sides. Swirling the wine will vaporize many of the odors and make them more available to the taster.

A Question of Taste

Taste is fairly simple to determine and is an enormous factor in defining the quality of a wine (hence, the use of the word "taste" for all aspects of organoleptics). Although only four tastes are discernable in wine, they tell a lot about how the wine was made, the conditions of the fruit and the age of the wine. The degree of sourness relates to total acidity (TA) and volatile acidity (VA) which will be discussed later in the book. Bitterness is usually the result of tannins in the wine, but may rarely be caused by microbial infection which is discussed toward the end of the book. The perception of saltiness in wine is always slight, but in greater amounts is associated with contamination. While sweetness is never *caused* by a fault, it may be present as the result of a winemaker attempting to cover one up.

The F̶o̶u̶r̶ Five Tastes and How Wine Affects Them.

The human mouth has over 10,000 taste buds. Every part of the tongue has receptors for the basic five tastes.

Is the traditional tongue map misleading?

Yes... well somewhat. We do sense all of the following five tastes everywhere on our tongue, but some tastes are more intensely felt in certain locations (such as sourness on the sides of our tongues).

The misconception is the result of a poor translation of German research that took place over a century ago and has persisted in the public mind until recently (Collins 1974).

The mouth is host to the sensations of taste, smell and touch. When we eat or drink, what are known as tastants enter our mouth. These are the chemicals in the food or drink and they become associated with our saliva. These various chemicals instantly find their way onto the taste cells and through an amazing series of connections register in the brain.

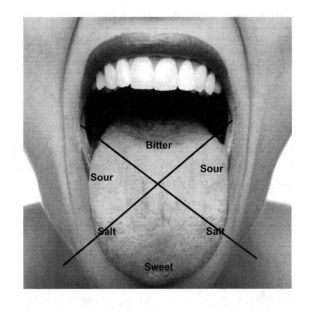

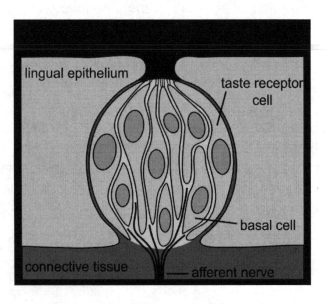

NEUROtiker, Wikimedia.

Wine Flaws and the Five Tastes

Sour: Probably the most survival-oriented taste ability we have, the sensation of sour is very important for determining quality and flaws such as *Volatile Acidity*, and works through *ion channels*, receptors which are sensitive only to sour and salty tastes.

Bitter: Another survival-oriented taste ability, which in wine is associated with tannins and SO_2 flaws.

Sweet: Like bitter and umami, sweet is signaled through G protein-coupled receptors. This taste is a flaw where style dictates dryness.

Salty: Rarely important in wine tasting except in denatured wine. Like sour, this flavor works through *ion channels*.

Umami: (Japanese for "Savory" or "Tasty") The taste of salts of glutamic acids or glutamates associated with MSG, are not associated with wine tasting so far.

旨味

Why we salivate

Saliva, slightly alkaline, contains enzymes that break down foods, and also distributes the taste to all of the tongue.

Mucus from the nose does the same, guaranteeing that even a few molecules of fragrance will be captured and sensed by the fine collecting hairs of the olfactory lining.

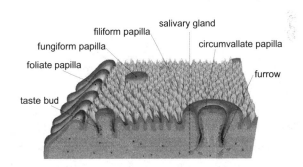

Smell and How it Works

The most complex of our senses is smell. Unlike appearance and taste, most odors are less definite in our minds. They are not just on a continuum of being distinguishable or not, but change with intensity and blend with other odors to create what the French first identified as "bouquet." The following is a description of how we smell, at what levels we distinguish odors and what accounts for the immense complexity of odors in wine.

How the nose detects odors:

The nose detects odors via a small bulb of nasal tissue 10 square centimeters (4 square inches). Making up only 5% of your nasal cavity, the olfactory bulb contains about 10 million odor receptor cells.* A volatile molecule fits into the shapes of some of the receptor cells, causing them to send signals to some of the 2,000 micro bunches (called glomeruli), which amplify the intensity of the signal along the olfactory tract to both the limbic system (primitive brain) and neocortex. The combined odor patterns are matched to one of the 10,000 odor memory patterns in your brain to either incite you to write a laboriously long book about lime-blossom tea and Madeleines[§] or to exclaim, "this Cabernet Sauvignon is full of pyrazines!"

* In dogs, this olfactory lining is 170 cm with 100 times more receptors per-square centimeter!
[§] Thanks to Proust 1919.

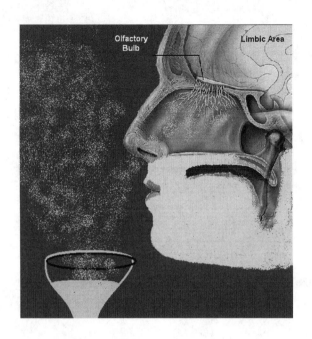

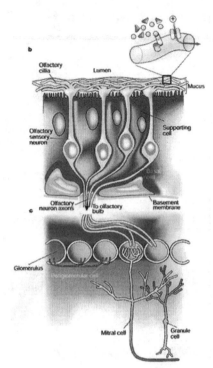

Neural pathways in the Olfactory
Bulb (Stuart Firestein, 2001)

Sensitivity

The lowest concentration at which a compound can be detected is called the **Odor Threshold**. The lower the odor threshold, the stronger the odorant. Grapefruit odor (1-p-menthene-8-thiol), for instance, can be detected at .1 ppt. That's .1 part-per-trillion; or *1 part-per-ten-trillion*; or .1 nanogram per liter (.1 ng/l); or 1/1,000,000ᵗʰ of a gram in a metric ton of water. **Perception Threshold** is the concentration at which 50% of tasters can distinguish the odorant. The minimum concentration at which an odor can be identified is referred to as the **Recognition Threshold**.

Odor Activity Value (OAV)

Also called "flavor activity," this measures how much an odorous compound will affect the bouquet of a solution.

$$OAV = \frac{Concentration}{Threshold}$$

This can vary. For example, in Bulgarian rose oil, citronellol is 270 times more abundant than β-damasceone but has only four times the effect on the bouquet.

Rose Oil Componet	% of Oil	Threshold in PPB	OAVs × 10³	Rel. % of OAVs
(-)-Citronellol	38	40	9500	4.3
β-Damascenone	0.14	0.002	156000	19.2

The following table includes just a few of the odorants from an Okanagan oak-aged Chardonnay and demonstrates how their different concentrations and thresholds can affect the overall bouquet. These compounds are generated from three sources: the grape variety, which for our Chardonnay produces damascenone (apple, rose and honey); fermentation, i.e. ethyl hexanoate and isoamyl alcohol, the first giving a fruity, apple peel and strawberry smell and the latter giving a rather unpleasant burnt, whisky, bitter smell; and finally, the oak-contributed odors such as vanillin and furfural (in this case their high thresholds probably contributed nothing to the bouquet of the wine).

Chardonnay Component	Threshold ug/L	Concentration ug/L	OAV
B-Damascenone	0.002	3	1500
Ethyl Hexanoate	1	600	600
Isoamyl Alcohol	300	50000	167
Vanillin	20	150	3
Furfural	3000	100	.003

(Tables from Nigel Eggers at www.perfspot.com/docs/doc.asp?id=40901)

What is it that you are smelling?

There are probably more than a thousand chemical compounds in wine. Of those, more than 200 are volatile active aroma compounds (Hartman 2003). They are found in the following functional groups:

- alcohols
- volatile acids
- esters
- terpenes
- sulfur compounds
- phenols
- lactones
- nitrogen compounds
- heterocyclic compounds

Some of these volatiles have become characteristic of specific varietal wines and are expected at high concentrations. For example terpenes and esters are associated with Rieslings, Muscats and other "floral" wines, usually as a result of fermentation (Sacks 2010). Other organic volatiles such as oak lactones enter the wine through later treatment.

A Question of Taste or Odor?

Because taste and odor are closely related, the two senses can be difficult to distinguish. To test which one you are experiencing, pinch off your nostrils with your fingers. Swirl the wine in your mouth. What you sense is the "taste" and feel—through mechanoreceptors and other exteroceptive senses—of the wine.

In the mouth the vapors circulate around the uvula or return up the esophagus after swallowing and into the nasal cavity. This is called "retro-nasal" sensing and may stimulate odors different from those detected by the nose orthonasally.

Professional wine tasters spit when judging numerous wines to avoid inebriation although, unavoidably, some of the alcohol is absorbed in the mucus membrane of the mouth and nose. Swallowing only a few drops of the wine will impart more information about the wine bouquet retro-nasally.

Factors Influencing Smell and Taste

There are several factors that influence your perception of taste which should always be kept in mind. They fall into two categories:

Idiosyncratic	Situational
Age	Adaptation (from repetition)
Illness (and affects of medication)	The Power of Suggestion
Cultural Background/ State of Mind	Environmental/Contextual
Color Perception	
History of smoking	

Components of Wine and Their Interactions

Wine, like everything we drink—even water—is a combination of chemicals, salts and metals. Unlike water, wine has a myriad of constituents, numbering in the hundreds if not thousands. Most of these components we cannot taste or even detect reliably through chemistry. It is the combined effect of different concentrations of components that accounts for the different tastes among wines.

Alcohols

Alcohols are a large chemical group and important in wine for a number of reasons:

- They greatly affect the taste of the wine (from hot to sweet to bitter).
- They play a role by combining with acids during fermentation—and subsequent maturation—to create a variety of esters.
- They also combine with oxygen to create acetaldehyde (see section on High Brix, High Alcohol pg. 20).

Ethanol: The predominant alcohol found in wine.

Methanol: A smaller molecule than ethanol. It boils at lower temperature and is harmful when in larger quantities than are naturally found in wine.

Propanol: Rubbing alcohol. More than 15 g. will get you sick, not drunk.

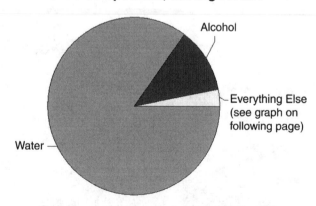

Wine Composition, The Big Picture

Alcohol

Everything Else (see graph on following page)

Water

Graphs used with permission of Andrew L. Waterhouse Copyright 2002, 2004, 2005

10

Higher alcohols or fusel alcohols:
Larger molecules than ethanol. They boil at higher temperatures. Examples are isoamyl and isobutyl alcohol.

Glycerol: A polyol related to alcohol. After ethanol it is the most abundant component in wine. It becomes important at >5% in dry wines, when it is thought to impart mouthfeel and what is sensed as a mild "sweetness."

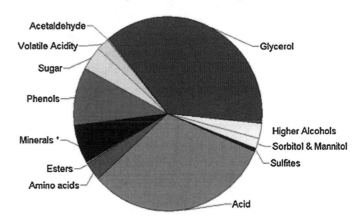

Red Wine Composition, Minor Components

Graphs used with permission of Andrew L. Waterhouse
Copyright 2002, 2004, 2005

Fixed Acids

Tartaric acid and malic acid are the most abundant in wine. Other acids that might affect the taste include citric, lactic, succinic and pyruvate.

Volatile Acidity (VA)

VA is the total concentration of all the volatile acids in a wine. Most of the VA is attributed to acetic acid. In very small amounts VA can add complexity, but otherwise VA along with ethyl acetate (nail polish smell) are faults. White wines and rosés exhibit VA less often than reds because of the manner in which they are fermented.

- VA is perceptible at 0.8 g/l.
- It has a definite vinegar flavor above 1.5 g/l.
- Normal wines contain 0.3–0.6 g/l acetic acid.
- The EU limit is 1.08 g/l for whites; reds 1.2 g/l.

Volatile Acidity is especially a problem in hot-climate wines, and can increase as wines age in the bottle.

Residual Sugar (RS)

RS is the total amount of sugar in grams per liter remaining after fermentation. Winemakers often leave residual sugar in the wine. Most grape sugar is in the six-carbon form of glucose and fructose at the time of fermentation, however some five-carbon sugars (eg: arabinose, rhamnose and xylose) are non-fermentable, so they remain in the wine, adding some body and taste. Wines fermented to dryness often contain 2–5 g/l residual sugar.

Inversion: In the presence of acids, enzymes or heat, sucrose is converted (hydrolyzed) to glucose and fructose.

Phenolics (Polyphenols)

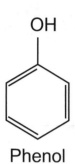

OH

Phenol

Several hundred polyphenols affect the taste, color and mouthfeel of any wine. These come mostly from the skin of the grape, but also from the seeds and oak (if oak is used). Polyphenols associated with color (anthocyanins) probably serve to protect the grape from ultraviolet radiation, insects and fungus. Phenolics fall under two categories:

- Non-Flavonoids, such as resveratrol (the life-extending antioxidant)
- Flavonoids, which include tannins, anthocyanins, flavonols and catechins compounds from the grape.

Minerals

In finished wine, potassium, sodium, phosphorous, magnesium and calcium are found in the greatest quantities, but dozens of other minerals also add to the taste of the wine. It is argued that the mineral content of an individual vineyard's soil can make its grapes taste different from those of the same variety grown at a different location. In France this site-specific flavor is known as *"gout de terroir."*

TA *vs* pH

Because acids are such an important component of wine, a discussion on how these are measured is essential. One measurement relates to taste while the other relates to a wine's stability. Acids, in turn have an effect on a wine's longevity. Wine is a "living substance" both biologically and chemically; therefore, it changes through time. Many of the faults described in this book are slow to develop in the bottle. Total Acidity (TA, or titratable acidity) is a measurement by volume (and therefore percentage) of the amount of all fixed acids in a liter of wine. TA will usually fall between 4.5 g to 13 g per liter. (Some labs use one-tenth of a liter—100 ml as the sample—in which case the TA runs between .45 g and 1.3 g.) The majority of this acid is malic and tartaric, with citric and succinic representing a much smaller portion.

TA is often described as "what we taste" in acid. A wine with a 5 g/L TA is usually quite flat and "flabby." A wine with 9 g/L TA is usually very acidic and "sharp" tasting (but residual sugar in a wine can ameliorate that sharpness).

Through conductivity a pH meter can measure the power of the hydrogen ion in these acids. This is a measure of a wine's "stability," or, the ability to inhibit the growth of unwanted microbes and avoid chemical change. A high pH (close to 4.0) is *very unstable,* and a low pH (close to 3.0) is *very stable.*

While there is an inverse correlation between TA and pH—high pH usually means low TA—it is not a consistent relationship. It is possible to have a must with high pH and high TA which is quite problematic and common in some hybrid-based wines from the eastern United States. In this case, acidity must be reduced using a double salt method, which will lower the total acidity of the wine faster than it increases the pH. ($CaCO_3$ will precipitate out the potassium with hydrogen.) The acidity can be adjusted later by adding acid to the wine. (For other methods see Walker 2002).

How do acids decrease after veraison?

While the process is not totally understood, malic acid tends to diminish after veraison. This is likely related to cell respiration and other metabolic activities associated with fruit ripening. High temperatures activate enzymes that catabolize malic acid (Jackson 2008:83).

While tartaric acid is more stable, it changes form as potassium uptake increases during ripening. After veraison, as long as there is soil moisture, the vine's root tips absorb potassium and pump it up to the berries, where a portion of it combines with free tartaric acid to form calcium tartarate, further elevating the pH of the grape (Boulton 2010 and ibid). Potassium Ions (K+) exchange with Hydrogen Ions (H+) raising the pH and indirectly lowering the Total Acidity. This is a major cause of low TAs and high pHs in warm harvest locations.

Warning

Volatile Acidity is becoming a common problem in warmer climate wine-producing areas because of the high sugar content of the grapes (resulting in high alcohol content) and the generally high pH of the musts. High pH may lead to development of acetic acid, which, when coupled with high alcohol (discussed later in this book) will produce ethyl acetate—a vintner's worst nightmare. Of the 60 Cabernet Sauvignons from Eastern Washington State tested and tasted in a recent study, almost one-third had taste-detectable VA as a flaw or fault and 40% had ethyl acetate over 200 mg/L. or acetic acid levels of over 700 mgs/liter (Hudelson, from Mumma et al. 2009).

Vive le Vin! Toward a "Living" Model for Wine

Everyone in the industry knows that wine is a "living substance," but what does that mean? Wine evolves? Chemical mixtures change with time, usually in the ratios of one compound to another. Pure ethanol mixed with distilled water will slowly evaporate, changing the original ratio in favor of water. The odor and taste effect of this change is a diminished intensity of the alcohol smell and taste. (This process is part of the secret of barrel-aging distilled spirits.)

Most changes in wine after it is bottled affect not just intensity, but also quality. Wine has more than 700 compounds (Jackson 2010:271). Most of these are aromatic and contribute to the overall flavor of the wine. However, the odor threshold is far too high for most of these compounds to be detected at the concentrations in which they occur in wine.

But the story does not end there. Some compounds break down or volatilize with time, often the most aromatic esters. Others, like tannins and long proteins, precipitate out of solution. In this sense, wine is chemically "living." Add to this that all but the most sterile filtered wines (and probably those as well) have micro-organisms that affect the wine soon after bottling and sometimes for years (as in the case of *Brettanomyces* and *Zygosaccharomyces bailii*). Yeasts and other microbes are organized bundles of enzymes, constantly breaking apart sugars, acids and other compounds for the benefit of cell survival. The most common flaw resulting from these organisms in wine is the presence of volatile acids.

In addition to their product, when those micro-organisms die, their structures, in turn, break down, changing further the composition, and maybe the taste, of the wine. The only governors in this process are the antiseptic effects of alcohol and SO_2, which destroy organisms and limit oxygen availability. Luckily for humans, most of these changes are beneficial and "to our taste."

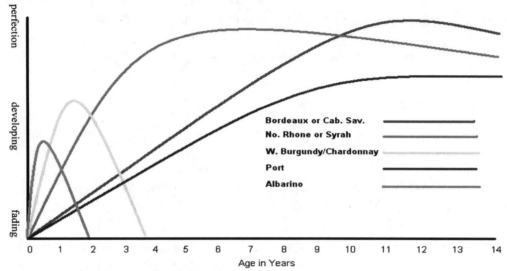

Bordeaux or Cab. Sav.	————————
No. Rhone or Syrah	————————
W. Burgundy/Chardonnay	————————
Port	————————
Albarino	————————

Development in the Bottle of Different Wines from a Great Vintage
(following Johnson/Robinson 07)

The Masking of Flavors and Faults

Because of their complexity, almost all wines have components we would describe as flaws if we could smell them; however, they are masked by more positive odiferous components. Even the taste of sourness can be masked by sugar in a wine.

The most important concept for understanding wine faults (and flavors) is the effect of "masking." Stronger odors, usually with higher OAVs, will overpower lesser odors. Such is the theory used in the production of the automobile deodorizers that hang from many rearview mirrors. A more complex process occurs when certain odors actually block other odors apparently "neutralizing" them. This is sometimes referred to as "cross adaptation" (Jackson 2008:661). While the physical process is not well understood, it is possible that nasal receptors are filled, or their signals blocked, by the OAV of a different compound. This is thought to be what happens when wine becomes "reduced" and volatile sulfur compounds (VSC) dominate. The fruity odor of the wine will be the first to "disappear." One may, or may not, smell the VSCs—in the form of H_2S or Mercaptans—but, the fruit will be masked by them. If the wine is treated to lower the concentration of VSCs, the fruit odors and flavors will return.

The same is true for odors associated with the green pepper smells of isobutyl methoxypyrazine. They will, in very low concentrations, mask fruit flavors.

What am I masking?

14

Even more subtle—and very important—is the additive effect of odors in wine. Two or more odors whose individual concentrations are below our detectable odor thresholds, may nevertheless set off a combined detectable signal when filling numerous nasal receptor cells at the same time.

The importance of these odor interactions cannot be overstated. The concept of "masking" can be a tool for the wine maker. The oxidized metallic smell of acetaldehyde if only slightly detectable, can be lessened by adding SO_2 which binds with the aldehydes and keeps them from being volatile. This is only a partial solution because acetaldehyde—detectable or not—can contribute to hangover if not general allergic reactions (often caused by cheap wines).

The masking effect can also be a liability. As will be discussed later, some VSCs such as methanethiol—which smells like stagnant water—when oxidized prior to bottling will become dimethyl disulfide with a much higher sensory threshold. If that threshold is high enough that the volatile sulfur cannot be detected the vintner may think it has disappeared, especially after a vigorous racking. In the more oxygen-starved environment of the bottle, the chemistry may reverse and methanethiol's rotten odor may re-emerge.

Finally, there are taste compounds that add "quality" to a wine's flavor and/or stability but, in high doses, mask more complex flavors. Various tannins are the culprits here, but the petrol aroma/taste found in Rieslings can do the same.

Most wines—including the *Premiers Grands Crus Classés* from Bordeaux—probably contain many horrible-smelling compounds, but in such low concentrations that they fall far below our human detection and are masked by more appealing attributes. This leads us to a simple truism for wine faults in general: ***It's the dose that makes the poison***.

A Descriptive Key for Determining Faults

Taste and smell are very subjective inquiries and vary enormously in human populations. It is hoped that the following taxonomic key will be a springboard for more accurate versions created by more sensitive eyes, palates and noses.

	White Wine	**Red Wine**
Appearance		
Bubbles	Refermentation of residual sugar (p. 5). LAB (pp. 48–50)	Same as for white wine
Cloudy	Charged solids (p. 5). Casse (p. 33) Bacteria (p. 52)	Non-fined red or same as for white wine
Off-Color	pH & age relevant, (p. 5). Laccase (p. 20). Oxidation (p. 40)	Relevant to pH of wine (p. 4). Oxidation (p. 40)
Deposits	White crystals—tartaric acid. Granules – microbes (p. 53) Oily – "ropiness,"—various microbes (p. 52) Surface deposits—"flowers", various microbes (p. 52)	Purple/black covers bottle – anthocyanins (p. 5/56). Ropiness—More common problem in reds (p. 52). Surface deposit—same, less common in reds (p. 52).

Odor and Taste

Hot/Burning	Entire nose & mouth—high ethanol (p. 22) Mostly nose, back of throat—SO**2**, CO**2** (p. 45). Hot acids, back of throat—see "acidic" below.	Same as white wine but compounded with bitter. SO**2**—burn **less** obvious in red wine. Back of throat—VA **more** obvious in red wine.
Acidic/Vinegary	Back of throat—acetic acid (p. 46) Sweet & sour—lactic souring (p. 52) Sauerkraut—*Candida stellata* (p. 52)	Same as white; acetic acid more obvious in red Same as white. Same as white.
Bitter	Fusel oil—amyl alcohol (p. 22) Bitter & acidic—amertume (p. 52) Bitter almonds—laccase (p. 20).	Side of tongue, gums; harsh tannins not in white. Amertume same in reds. Laccase rare in reds
Butteriness, rancid butter	Diacetyl—A byproduct of malolatic fermentation Off flavor: MLB's effect on citric acid (pp. 48–50).	Not considered a good flavor in reds.
Metallic	"Green apple/old wine taste"—oxidation (p. 40) Metallic odors—*Brettanomyces* (p. 51)	Less common smell in red—but see "Off Color" Same in reds
Plastic/ Acetate	Acetone, fingernail polish—Ethyl acetate (pp. 22–23, 46) With ropiness (above)—microbic spoilage (p. 52)	Same as for whites. Ropiness same in reds.
Green	Bell pepper—methoxypyrazines, rare in whites (p. 21) Harsh vegetal—MALB (p. 20) Geranium—Malolactic effect on sorbate (p. 53)	Bell pepper methoxypyrazines, green fruit. (p. 21) Same for reds Same for reds—also result of MLB (p. 53).
Moldy	Old sofa/wet cardboard—TCA (pp. 35–36) Wet cardboard/wet wool—Light Strike (p. 54) Mushrooms: Laccase, Sufur and Geosim (pp. 20, 54) Wet towel/ dish rag/mothballs—ATA (p. 53)	TCA—same in reds as whites. Light strike rare in Reds Laccase less common in Reds ATA not common in red wines.
Mousy, Bandaid Barnyard, Horsey	"Smoky-spicy"—*Ethyl-4-guaiacol* plus "Leather, horsey"—*Ethyl-4-phenol* becomes Band-aid!—*Vinyl-4-phenol* (p. 51)	Putrid: biogenic amines (p. 54). Much more common in red wine than white.
Sulfur/Egg-like	Rotten egg smell—H_2S (For all of these: pp. 39–43). Cooking gas—mercaptans Cabbage—methyl mercaptan Cooked corn—dimethyl sulfide Rubbery—diethyl sulfide Garlic/burnt rubber—diethyl disulfide	Also, TDN (p. 56). Same in reds as whites for all.

It Came From the Vineyard…
(or some other place).

Courtesy P.Sholberg, Agriculture & AgriFood Canada

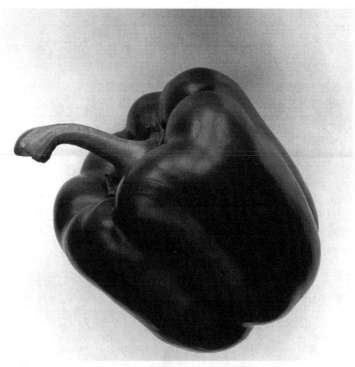

*This illustration was made by **Luc Viatour***

Wine is not made in the vineyard much anymore. Natural wine, made from wild vines may have pleased our Neanderthal ancestors, but it would not be acceptable to most of us today. Grapes are one of the most "cultured"—or "messed with"—of fruits. This and the following section deal with that fact: both nature and man sometimes add too little and sometimes too much for the result to be a flawless wine.

Over the past 6,000 years we humans have selected for the best grape clones and crossed them with each other, sometimes accidentally, to produce several thousand varieties that make excellent wine. In fact, we did not just develop their gene pools, but we even altered the way grapes grow. In the wild, the genus *Vitis* (representing all grapes) grows under large trees, so as to use them as scaffolding to gain height. The fruit of these vines is sparse, low in sugar and "green" tasting. Green vegetativeness is also the taste one gets when a commercial vineyard allows the grapes to become covered by foliage all season.

So, there is little *natural* about growing good wine. Even in the best of climates, vines must be sprayed for fungus and insects if one wants good healthy fruit. Therein lies another problem. Too much spray at the wrong time can leave residuals on the fruit that can affect fermentation results Too little spray often results in moldy fruit creating poor quality wine with off-odors.

In addition to those horticultural problems, too little nitrogen absorption by the grape—a result of over-cropping, insufficient sunlight or poor soils—will result in "stuck fermentations." In this case, the human must take action again—with the addition of yeast nutrients.

The most common faults in today's major wine-producing regions arise from over-ripeness of fruit. While many vineyardists believe that long hang-time and shriveled grapes add a "fruit-bomb" character to the wine—a character that is popular among some critics—the ultimate product for those wines is low natural acids and high alcohol. Although low acids and high alcohols can be adjusted at the winery, there are concomitant problems associated with them. Later in this section, suggestions are given on how to judge when grapes are at their highest potential for good wine.

"It Came from the Vineyard" also covers the most common faults resulting from poor horticultural decisions. Aside from this, it is not a directive on how to grow good grapes, but an explanation for what might have caused many of the flaws that are described in the book.

Problems in Vine Physiology that Result in Faults

Nutrition Related Faults

Many wine faults turn out to be related to problems in fermentation, and the most common culprit is a deficiency of YAN.

YAN = Yeast Available (assimilable) Nitrogen—ammonium plus all free amino acids (except proline)

> *Grape nitrogen (N) status is crucial for successful winemaking….*
> *Wine yeast[s] require at least 140 mg/L of yeast assimilable amino-N (YAN) to*
> *complete fermentation (Agenbach, 1977). Low levels of must YAN can cause*

> *slow or stuck fermentations (Bisson, 1999). To compensate for low YAN, some wine-makers add diammonium phosphate (DAP) to their must. However, yeast will preferentially assimilate free ammonium ions over amino acids which can reduce the complexity and desirable flavor aromas of wine (Bisson and Butzke, 2000). Therefore a problem can exist if desirable low vigor leads to undesirable low must YAN concentrations.* —Stockert and Smart 2008

In the study quoted above, researchers found that some rootstocks that are popular in Eastern Washington because of their stunted shoot growth can result in less that one-half the YAN required for a complete fermentation. Such stress in fermentation leads to H_2S and sometimes forms volatile acidity if yeast nutrients are not added.

What are **other** causes of low YAN in grapes?

- Overcropping (more than 4 tons/acre in most soils)
- Lack of seasonal heat and sun
- Diseases, such as *Botrytis* and leaf roll virus.

The **Cure**: diammonium phosphate should be added to any must suspected of have low YAN.

Disease-related faults

Botrytis cineria produces laccase enzyme, which can oxidize a wide range of grape phenols (including reseveratrol, anthocyanins and tannins). It can also oxidize benzyl alcohol to benzaldehyde (bitter almond taste).

The worst result of *Botrytis c.* is that it encourages other microorganisms, such as acetobacter, which create taste flaws.

Tom Maack 2005 Wikimedia Commons

Insect-related faults

Multicolored Asian Lady Beetle (*MALB*) can ruin a wine. If there are as few as two lady beetles per lug (24 lbs), the resulting juice (wine) will be high in methoxy-pyrazines, which the beetles synthesize.

> *"Fly away home, your house is on fire so get the hell out of my vineyard!!"*

Other pests include Grape Berry Moth, a major problem east of the Mississippi, which can rot the inside of tight bunches of berries.

Bruce Marlin 2005 Wikimedia Commons

Green Flavors and Flaws

While the green flavors of under ripe grapes are sometimes a problem in cold climates, for most of the wine-producing world, green flavors in red wine are almost always the result of pyrazines. A slight scent of the green-pepper used to be associated with good Bordeaux wine in the past, today's fruit-driven wines tend to eschew the odor.

Recent research on the pyrazine issue—mostly in cool climates where it is more common—have literally thrown light on the problem. Leaf pulling, shoot thinning and hedging have served to put the fruit in the sunlight, reducing the pyrazines.

Methoxypyrazines

Herbaceous, "green" aromas, often associated with bell pepper, are acceptable in small doses. These odors are associated with some varieties more than others: Carmenere and Sauvignon blanc in particular (Belancic and Agosin, 2007) and Cabernet Sauvignon. Most green aromas in red wines, however, are associated with a lack of direct sun on the berries from berry set until shortly before veraision.

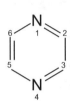

Pyrazines in general are heterocyclic compounds similar to histamines and found in many foods, most commonly chocolate and coffee.

3-isobutyl-2-methoxypyrazine (IBMP)

Some other pyrazines found in wine:

2-Ethylpyrazine C6H8N2	Nutty, walnut, roasted, buttery, musty, woody, peanut butter
5,6,7,8- Tetrahydroquinoxaline C8H10N2	Coffee, cheese, sweet roasted nut
2,3-Diethylpyrazine C8H12N2	Nutty, hazelnut, cereal, earthy, fungi, potato, meaty
3-Ethyl-2- methoxypyrazine C7H10N2O	Roasted nut, hazelnut, earthy
3-Ethyl-2-acetylpyrazine	Potato chip, popcorn, nutty, meaty
3-Isopropyl-2- methoxypyrazine C8H12N2O	Earthy, bell pepper, potato, vegetable
3-Sec-butyl-2- methoxypyrazine C9H14N2O	Green bell pepper
3-Isobutyl-2- methoxypyrazine C9H14N2O	Green bell pepper

From Hartmann 2003

High Brix, High Alcohol and Balance Faults

Brix is a measure of sugar in grapes. A high Brix level can lead to a high alcohol level. High sugar content does not inherently make a flawed wine; however, the common correlation between high sugar at late berry ripeness and depletion of malic acids in warm climate vineyards does create difficulties. The high pH of hot climate fermentations creates greater opportunities for spoilage microbes to affect wine quality and stability. In addition, it often leaves wines unbalanced, without sufficient "acid backbone" to counteract high fruitiness or sweetness.

Alcohol is an important ingredient in the "mouth-feel" of a wine. High alcohol wines (arbitrarily let's say above 14% for table wines) are often harsh on the finish, burning the back of the palate. One of the most common misconceptions of novice winemakers is that high alcohol content will give a wine stability. As will be seen in the following pages it is often the opposite. Alcohol in high-pH musts and wines offers fuel for microbes and enzymes to degrade a wine rapidly.

Higher Alcohols in Wine

Esterification and Hydrolysis

Ethanol is not the only alcohol resulting from high-sugar musts. Higher alcohols will have more than two carbons and are often result in odors or odiferous esters. With the exception of 2 phenolethanol, which has a honey, spice, rose-like fragrance, most higher alcohols do not have pleasant odors. Isoamyl alcohol, one of the most common, is described as bitter and burnt. But the same alcohol is a precursor to isoamyl acetate (banana smell). Glycerol, sometimes referred to as a higher alcohol, gives body and mouth feel to wines.

Alcohols play a big role in the development of esters that add fruitiness and floral components to the "nose" of a wine. Esters are formed by the combination of two reactants, an alcohol and an acid.

The reverse of this reaction is hydrolysis. Water with the catalyst NaOH will change the ester back to an acid (usually carboxylic) and alcohol. Because these are equilibrium processes, the degree of stability depends on concentrations of the ingredients.

Good Esters Bad Esters

Esters are odorous derivaties of acids, alcohols and phenols resulting from fermentation. They can be beneficial to the qualities in the wine. The fatty acid esters that result from some fermentations can add pleasant odors—ethyl butanolate (apple peel) and ethyl hexanoate (strawberry). Finally, one of the most common results of this process involves ethanol. In the presence of acetic acid, ethanol will convert to ethyl acetate (the smell of fingernail polish remover), a major flaw. The obvious way to guard against such degeneration is to minimize the production of acetic acid.

Ethyl Acetate

Ethyl butyrate

Polyols

Polyhydric alcohols (sometimes called "sugar alcohols") are higher alcohols that include the above "fusel oils" and glycerol (the most abundant higher alcohol and most important for mouth feel). Manitol, erythritol, aribitol, sorbitol and others of this group are usually a result of fructose reduction and are found in greater amounts in fruit affected by *botrytis* and other molds. In small amounts they add to the complexity of late-harvest wines but can also contribute to bitter, flawed wines.

Two products with glycerin...hmmm

glycerin

Another Sensory Problem Resulting from Alcohol

Acetaldehyde represents 90% of the aldehydes found in wine. While it is a by-product of fermentation, most of the acetaldehyde found in wine is the result of ethanol oxidation (by the same enzyme that is found in your body). In small amounts it can add complexity to wine. In some sherries it is a dominant feature of the style. In most wines, high amounts (>150 mg/l) of acetaldehyde create problems. Descriptions include *"green apples, sour, metallic, flat, tired, maderized."*

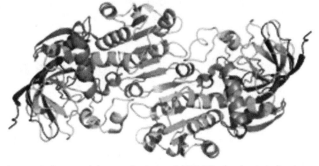

A crystallographic rendering of ADH5 alcohol dehydrogenase enzyme converting alcohol to acetaldehyde (Emw-wikimedia)

In the body, acetaldehyde is created from alcohol by the enzyme alcohol dehydrogenase, which exists naturally in the liver. Acetaldehyde is toxic but the liver further metabolizes it to produce a harmless acetate. This requires glutathione and the enzyme acetaldehyde dehydrogenase. A lack of either will cause the effects of hangover or worse. Some individuals have low levels of the enzyme, a condition that is often genetic or gender-related but can also be caused purposely by taking the drug antabuse to block the enzyme's production.

The presence of SO_2 during fermentation contributes to acetaldehyde production. Adding it after fermentation hides the taste effects, but not the chemical effects. (*http://www.epa.gov/chemfact/s_acetal.txt*).

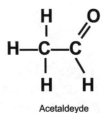

Acetaldeyde

Acetaldehyde levels in alcoholic beverages

Type	Acetaldehyde (mg/L)
Red Wine	4 – 212
White Wine	11 – 493
Sweet wine	188 – 248
Sherry	90 – 500
Brandy	63 – 308

Above table: Andrew L. Waterhouse as summarized from Liu *et al.* (2000).

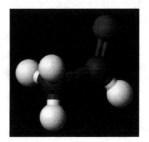

How to Avoid High Alcohol in the Winery

Sweet Wines

Even if the grape sugars are at 28 Brix, high alcohol can be avoided by leaving 4%–8% residual sugar in the finished wine. One must only be concerned about sufficient acidity (which can be added) and sterile filtering to avoid secondary fermentations. In such cases, sugar creates a more stabile environment than does alcohol.

Amelioration

Alcohol can be brought down to acceptable levels by adding water. The TTB allows one to bring down the must to 22 Brix prior to fermentation. California state law is more vague, and some countries have laws against any amelioration with water. These are almost always places where high sugar at harvest is not a problem.

Strangely, in the eastern USA, where high sugar is also not a problem, water may still be used. In this case, it is used to lower the acid level of the must. In all cases of amelioration, it is important to add the water prior to fermentation.

Removing Alcohol

This is done with spinning cones or cross-flow filtration (in which case it must be done at a distillery). The process is quite expensive. In addition to this, some yeasts have been selected for their propensity to increase the "higher alcohols," such as glycerol, and to avoid fermentation of some of the sugar to ethanol. Unfortunately, this often results in wines high in acetates as well as the desired glycerol.

Blending

The easiest way to avoid high alcohol is to blend low-sugar grapes to the problematically high-sugar must. This can also be done by blending low-alcohol finished wines to high-alcohol wines, but without the synergies created in a more stable fermentation. There is a bias in the western wine world that the grapes must be picked at the peak of their physiological maturity, when sugars are highest and often very little acid remains. The fact is, especially for white grapes from hot climates, one can pick at three to five degrees of Brix below the peak—when acids are still above 8 g./l.—without suffering "green" notes on the palate.

Overripe Grapes and High Alcohol

Determining the fruit's physiological maturity is important for good wine. Hang-time can rid grapes of undesirable characteristics such as the steminess of pyrazines. Too much hangtime can create overripe plummy flavors with low fixed acids, high pH and caustically high alcohol.

The following pages are to aid in deciding what is the optimal time for harvesting. Of course, this will vary according to variety—some are optimal at higher sugars than others—and style of wine. Pinot Noir and Chardonnay are harvested between 17 and 19 Brix in Champagne, between 20 and 22 Brix in Burgundy and between 22 and 24 Brix in California.

More than Brix meters (refractometers) or pH meters, the structure and taste of the skins, pulp and seeds will indicate ripeness. The following diagram visually shows sugar development and acid reduction during a normal season.

25

Parameters for Fruit Ripeness

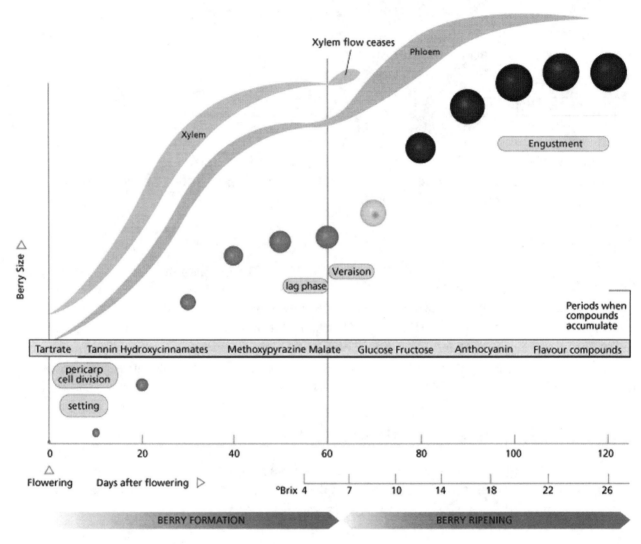

The above diagram shows relative size and color of berries at 10-day intervals after flowering, passing through major developmental events. Also shown are the periods when compounds accumulate, the levels of juice Brix, and an indication of the rate of inflow of xylem and phloem vascular saps into the berry. Illustration by Jordan Koutroumanidis, Winetitles.

Random Sampling of Grapes to Determine Optimal Ripeness

The score cards on the following page are useful for determining fruit ripeness. But in collecting a sample, it is most important to obtain what might be considered a "mean" for the ripeness of a block or vineyard and not an arbitrary sample of the ripest or the least ripe fruit for analysis.

Good sampling can easily be done by taking grapes equally from all parts of the chosen clusters—the wings, the body and the tip.

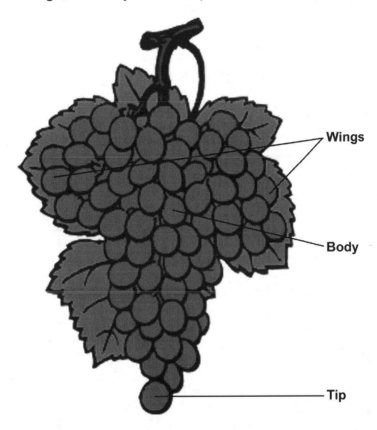

In addition, these clusters should be chosen as randomly as possible. If you are not using a calculator with a number generator that can help you randomize the row and vine number, then choose different vine numbers on every third row. On each chosen vine, sample one cluster near the trunk, one from half-way down the cordon (or cane) and one from the apical region of the cordon (or cane).

Evaluating Berry Readiness through Sensory Analysis

Visual—Tactile—Taste

Sample # 1	Grape Berry Development Post Veraison				
VISUAL	1	2	3	4	6
Color	Green	Dappled	Light-color	Brilliant	Dull-Dark
Attachment	Difficult	must hold pedicel	"pops off"	w/o holding pedicel	Falls off
Elasticity	Hard berry	Pops back	Pops back slowly	no elasticity	squishes
PULP TASTE	1	2	3	4	6
Juice	sour "meaty"	sweet "meaty"	pulp sticks to seeds	seeds free	all juice
Sugar	"green" tasting	sour	sweet	very sweet	alcoholic
SKINS	1	2	3	4	6
Toughness	hard to puncture	hard to shred	still piece	disintegrates	same as pulp
Skin Tannin	harsh/green	astringent	slightly astringent	warm round	none
SEEDS	1	2	3	4	6
Color	Green	Amber	Mottled	Brown	Dark
Seed Taste	Very Hard/Bitter	Bitter	Crackable "hoppy"	Crunchy/Coffee	mealy
Ripeness:	<14 weeks yet!	15–25 unripe	26–35 early ripeness	36–40 Ripe	>41 Rotten?

Color: Post-Veraison berries of the cluster will darken (for red) or go from green to glassy (for white). "Red" and "Blue" varieties will darken gradually filling in the cluster randomly, from the exposed side of the cluster to the "inside" shaded side of the cluster. The last part of the berry to darken is that which is closest to the stem.

Tactile: Two measures - how easily the berry pulls off the small stem (pedicel) and the softness of the berry. Squeeze the berry between the index finger and thumb: do the indentations remain?

Taste of Pulp: Randomly choose several berries to put into your mouth. Crush them on roof of mouth. Is the pulp gelatinous (sticking to the seeds) or "juicy?"
Is the fruit Sweet? Sour? Herbaceous? Fruity?

Push the seeds out of the pulp into your hand. Keep the skins in your mouth but spit or swallow the pulp

Skin Tasting: Chew the skins 16 times (the same for all samples). Do the skins stay tough? Becoming mush? Rub the chewed skins on the roof of your mouth with your tongue and then place between your upper lip and gum. When you rub your tongue along the roof of your mouth is it smooth or rough? Swallow or spit out the skins. Can you taste (your feel) the tannins along your upper gums?

Seed Tasting: How brown are the seeds in your hand? Gently chew on them. Are they bitter, green tasting, crunchy?

Adapted from Trioli and Rousseau, BSA, IVC

Wine Purity and Faults

Contaminants are all substances that are not naturally found in wine and that do not occur naturally as a byproduct of winemaking. *We cannot taste most contaminants.*

Contaminants are sometimes the result of wine making; copper, for example, is used because it binds with H_2S and Mercaptans to take away faults associated with reduction. But copper is easily fined out of wine to the legal concentration of .5 mg/l. PVPP (*Poly*-vinyl-*poly*pyrrolidone) is a polymer not naturally occurring in wine, but used in its fining. It has been determined to have no effect on the drinker. The same can be said about other fining agents—gelatin, isinglass, egg whites, silicon dioxide etc. Generally these adulterants "drop" out of the wine, and the residuals are minimal. Bulls' blood used to be used as a fining agent, but due to bovine diseases, its use has been made illegal in the EU.

Egg Whites

Bentonite

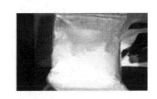

Casein

Isinglass

Bowler: Fisheries and Oceans Canada

Pesticide Residues

While residuals on grapes are often high, pesticides are rarely reported in wine (Cabras, 2001). Possibly we have not looked closely enough. A recent study analyzing 40 different wines from eight countries found that all but five of the wines (they were five of the six organic vineyards included in the study) had pesticide residues. The mean number of pesticides for each wine was 4, and a total of 24 different pesticides were detected. While most of the wines were "low cost affordable brands," three came from "world-class" Bordeaux wineries. One of those three had comparatively high levels of procymidone: a carcinogen, developmental/reproductive toxin and an endocrine inhibitor.

Although the Pesticide Action Network, which reported the findings, has reason for concern, the levels—most below 10 parts per trillion—were low, and most of the pesticides were not toxic. The highest residual reported by PAN was 233 ppt.

> *"Over one third of the total residues detected in the bottles of conventional European wines relate to fungicides recently adopted by European grape producers. A further third of residues identified relate to classes of fungicide whose use in grape production has escalated*

> *substantially over the past decade. The presence of these pesticides in conventional wines confirms the link between the escalating use of synthetic fungicides in European grape production and the changing nature of wine contamination."*   —PAN-Europe

Metals

Lead Poisoning/Saturnine Gout

High levels of lead was common in the wine of the Roman Era. It was a result of adding reduced (by boiling) grape juice called *sapa* or *defratum.* The reduction (by 1/2 or more) was often done in a lead pot (see left) which some have figured added up to 1 gram of lead per liter of wine. Some contemporary writers said it sweetened the wine.

Lead in today's wines?

The TTB reports that it randomly monitors metal ions in wine with a mass spectrometer and to date has "yet to detect any serious safety problems" (Wine Spectator 11/5/2008). The Liquor Control Board of Ontario Canada also tests for heavy metals and contaminants, and out of 8,000 products tested in the past 10 years, has only rejected eight for high levels of lead (ibid).

More Metals?

Metal Ions have been a recent concern in wine blogs. Declan Naughton, professor of biomolecular sciences and Andrea Petróczi, a sports and exercise scientist, both at Kingston University at London, found high levels of various metals in 13 out of 16 wines examined. The metals included iron, lead, copper, mercury, vanadium and manganese. Their study used secondary data from other researchers' findings, and applied EPA's Target Hazard Quotient (THQ), a risk estimation formula, which resulted in the following criticism:

> "It is important to note that THQ is a determination of long-term risk, the study added, and a typical 18-year-old would have to drink 8.5 ounces (one to two glasses) of the tested wines for more than 17,000 days before reaching a level of concern. This model also assumes that the same individual will live to be more than 80 years old."—Wine Spectator; ibid

Still, some of the wines had abnormally high THQ levels—350 for Slovakia and Hungary—where continued consumption of a THQ of >1 is considered dangerous. Wines from Argentina, Brazil and Italy were below a THQ of 1.

Metal Hazes

Using fermentation vessles of copper, zinc, iron or aluminum can cause hazes that are dark, brown, purple and even white. If the haze—called *casse*—is caused by iron or copper, a few drops of citric acid can usually solve the problem. If the haze is caused by zinc or aluminum, fining with egg whites and shells may work (see Fugelsang 2007 for procedures to determine metal hazes).

How do metals get into wine?

As with the Roman lead, the source can be the vessel used for mixing and fermenting. The source can also be metal pipes or tools. For about 150 years, copper, lead, arsenic and zinc were used as fungicides and sometimes entered the must, but rarely the wine. Below is a comparison of metal contamination from filter material. (Franson, 2008)

Metals (mg/kg Fining Agent)

	Arsenic	Cadmium	Chromium	Copper	Iron	Lead	Manganese	Mercury	Solenium	Silver	Zinc
Bentonite	3	<0.25	<0.25	<0.25	1015.6	3.1	1.2	<0.06	0.7	<0.25	17.55
D E	0.35	<0.25	3.25	<0.25	<2.5	<0.25	<0.25	<0.05	0.6	<0.25	0.25
Perite	<0.25	<0.25	<0.25	<0.25	<2.5	<0.25	0.45	<0.05	0.55	<0.25	0.25
Triex	<0.25	<0.25	<0.25	<0.25	<2.5	<0.25	<0.25	<0.05	0.55	<0.25	<0.25

Effects of Plastic

The degree that plastic is (or should be) used by the wine industry is a quandary. Its positive attributes are many. It is lightweight and more easily recycled than traditional materials. The most common concern is that it affects the flavor of the wine. There are five ways wine can be affected by plastics (each associated with different plastics). Not all of them are negative:

- **Taint:** Some vinyls (especially non-food grade PVC) impart plastic odors to wine. The same is true of epoxy resins (sometimes used as coatings on cement tanks) and styrene from fiberglass tanks, although the cases noted are rare (Jackson 2008:505).
  More important is that Bisphenol A, once found in Nalgene bottles (*throw away your old ones!*) and other PVC <3> plastics, may disrupt endocrine functioning.
- **Eliminating taint:** TCA (the cause of "corked wine") has an affinity for polyethylene plastic wrap (or milk cartons) which can absorb it from wine. The Burgundy-based company Boffim has developed an ionized copolymer with a similar effect.
- **Eliminating flavor:** Negative volatiles are not the only thing that can be absorbed by plastic. The ester octanoate and the terpene linalool (important flavor components of Muscat and Gewürztraminer) can be "scalped" by LDPE<4> and PP<3> (Sajilata 2007).

- **Gas Permeability:** If micro-oxygenation is what one wants, the permeability of an HDPE food grade tank can be helpful. One can choose the different thicknesses of tank walls for different rates of O_2 absorption in the wine and avoid expensive micro-oxygenation stones, barrels and barrel maintenance.
- **Oxidation of wine:** while there is a savings in shipping, PET <1> bottles are known to allow O_2 to diffuse into the wine at a rapid rate, giving white wine an oxidized flavor. More recently PET bottles and bag-in-the box wine bladders are being coated with a metallic fused polyester coextruded with ethyl vinyl alcohol (EVOH) to eliminate oxygen transfer (Goode 2006). This is not a problem for CO_2. Even the older PET bottles functioned well at maintaining CO_2 in sparkling wine.

Dangerous Adulterations

1984 would have been a good year for Austrian wine exports had scandals not broken out about 40 of its producers adding diethylene glycol (DEG), a toxic solvent, to their wines to create the ***perception of body and sweetness***. Several German wine producers were also implicated, and eventually DEG was said to be found in Banfi's Reunite brands (Cong. Ref. No. 90-3981X Filed: November 26, 1997). Although there were no deaths, the results were at first catastrophic to the Austrian wine industry. Exports of Austrian wine dropped 96% the next year. German exports suffered as well.

Diethylene glycol is not nearly as toxic as Ethylene Glycol (glycol: Greek "sweetly"). Several writers have claimed that the levels of DEG that appeared in the Austrian wines would require a person "to consume 28 of the bottles each day for at least two weeks for the ethylene glycol to have

The DEG formula diagram (right) is a palindrome.

an adverse effect" (http://www.foodreference.com). Still, decades earlier the Federal Food, Drug and Cosmetic Act in 1938 had been enacted because of the poisoning of 107 people by DEG, which was used in a "sulfa elixir" of the time. Even as late as February 2009, 84 children were reported to have died after being given teething syrup that contained the substance. (News.yahoo.com).

The Austrian wine producers who committed this crime may have believed that the solvent was harmless (even though not on a sanctioned list of additives). In fact, the way the scandal broke was that one producer listed DEG as a tax deduction. However, that they were trying to make "good wine" from bad should have generated remorse. The benefit that finally resulted is that the Austrian wine laws have become a model for strictness in the EU, and the wine industry was revamped at all levels of production including harvest limitations of tons per hectare in Austrian vineyards.

Methanol

Although methanol represents a very small percentage of the alcohols found in wine, unscrupulous vintners have used it to increase the body of their wine. In 1985 a scandal occurred in Italy after 24 people died and many others lost their sight from drinking cheap "Barbera" laced with methanol. The scandal was a setback for Italian wine exports for a couple of years, but not anything like what resulted from the diethylene glycol scandal of Austria.

Oops...

Not all contaminants added to wine are done so purposefully. Several years ago the author was asked to determine what the problem was with an 8,000-gallon tank of red wine that had turned quite salty and brackish and had high levels of ammonium salts. This particular brand of wine was usually artificially sweetened. What had happened? Apparently, a winery worker, thinking that he was dumping 40-pound bags of sugar into the cuvee, was accidentally adding the same amount of diammonium phosphate. It may not have been toxic, but it was definitely undrinkable.

Cork Taint and Cellar Taint

Although this is a "bio-induced" problem, it is a result of winemakers sometimes unwittingly contaminating their wines, and so, appears in this section of the book. The smell is usually considered similar to old sofa, wet washcloth, moldy newspaper and wet dog. Infected corks have most commonly been the cause. Because of changes in the industry, most cork suppliers claim that TCA (trichloral anisole) is found today in fewer than 1% of all corks. In 2005, the *Wine Spectator* tasting panel stated that 7% of the 2800 wines they tasted had some form of Tyrene (Fox, 2009). Although cork is the most common cause of this infection, lack of sanitation in the winery also contributes to the taint. To further confound the fault, the ability to detect these smells varies among tasters by 300 fold.

Tyrene, the smelly compound is detectable at 1.5–4 ppb, although the Australian Wine Institute has demonstrated that it can suppress a wine's bouquet at two parts-per-trillion. At that level it would only take a "good teaspoon full of pure TCA to spoil all the wine that is made in the USA" (Henick-Kling 2010). It has various forms depending on the chemical that the filamentous fungi (*Trichoderma longibrachiatum, Penicillium* spp., *Fusarium* spp., *Cladosporium* spp., and *Paecilomyces variotii*) interact with. Chlorine used to be the only concern, but more recently Bromines have become culprits in taint production. The results are 2,4,6-trichloroanisole (TCA) and 2,4,6-tribromoanisole (TBA). The latter is formed through the process of biomethylation of is precursor 2,4,6,TPB.

©2001 Andrew L Waterhouse
and UCD Students of Natural
Products of Wine

TCA

TBA

Avoiding Cork Taint

Most wineries by now have changed from chloride cleaners to peroxide or other detergents. Cork and oak companies have changed from Pentachloralphenol (PCP) insecticides (Jackson 2008:409) and chloro-(carbamate) bromine pesticides. However, there seem to be numerous other minor vectors for this repulsive smell, so elimination is far from at hand.

Reversing Cork Taint

Numerous techniques have been tried, including soaking polyethelene plastic (such as milk containers or plastic wrap) in the wine. The non-polar TCA has an affinity for the polyethelene. Using this technology, the Burgundy-based company Boffim has developed an ionized copolymer they call "Dream Taste" in the form of a small cluster of grapes that can be dropped into a decanter of tainted wine, ridding if of the odor. At $6 each, it adds considerably to the price of the bottle. G3, a company owned by Gallo, developed a metal-based filter that eliminates TCA but is quite costly. Some wine makers have used half and half to eliminate small doses; the milk fats are said to absorb the TCA. All of these are possible solutions, if the wine hasn't yet been bottled. If it has, start buying "Dream Taste" in large quantities.

It Grows in the Wine!

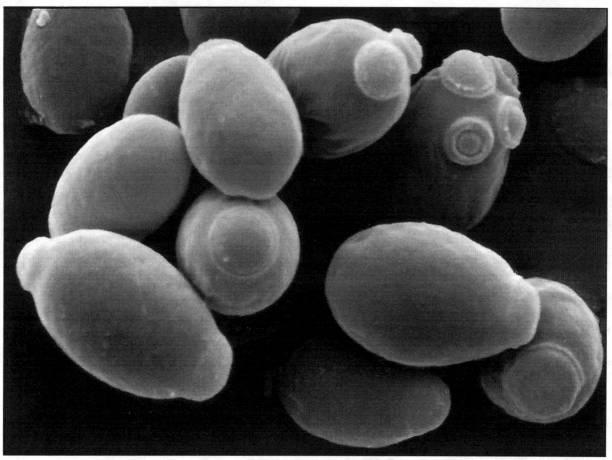

Zygosaccharomyces bailii **Mary Parker** Institute of Food Research, Norwich

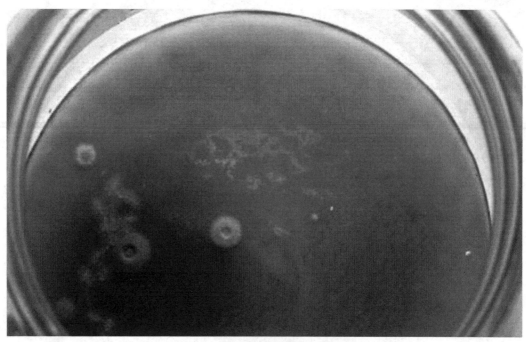

Nirinjan Singh, Wikimedia

Microbes, those invisible-to-the-naked-eye bacteria, yeast and molds that grow in must and wine, usually cannot be tasted. It is the substances that they produce that ruin the taste of a good wine. And even the good microbes like *Saccharomyces cerevisae,* which gives us the alcohol that distinguishes wine from grape juice, can impart rotten-egg gas under stressful conditions. This section concerns itself almost exclusively with the chemical faults created by microbes.

The section begins with a discussion of the oxidation-reduction process, the exchanging of electrons and oxygen. This process, often simply called redox, is essential to understanding how various smelly sulfur compounds get into wine.

Microbes are greatly affected by the pH of a wine. Generally speaking, the higher the pH of a wine, the more conducive it is to microbial growth. As was explained in the section "It Came from the Vineyard," the longer the hangtime of the grapes past optimal ripeness, the lower the natural acids and the higher the pH (not to mention high alcohol). These wines with high pH are much more difficult to guard against microbial infections.

Some microbes are essential to wine style. *Oenococcus oeni*, described on page 50, is used by the winemaker to convert malic acid to a softer lactic acid. This can add depth to a red wine, and it softens many high-acid white wines. This bacterium is preferred because it is the only type of lactic acid bacteria (LAB) that works at a low pH. It also produces fewer volatile acids than other LAB. But even *Oenococcus* produces some vinegary acetic acid and, in the wrong variety, such as Riesling, can ruin the desired crisp style sought in that wine. This section also deals with the numerous additional ailments associated with other bacteria, wild yeasts and even ultraviolet light waves.

Many faults can be traced to chemical precursors found in the grapes, which under the right conditions develop into off-flavors. Such is the case with atypical aging (ATA) and the petrol smell of TDN. This section ends with a discussion on these faults as well as problems arising from condensed tannins found in the skin, stems and seeds of the grape. Though they may serve many purposes—color retention, structure and longevity in the wine—as well as offering health benefits to humans, their most obvious expression is astringency, which above certain limits is seen as a fault.

Volatile Sulfur Compounds

Redox

A compound becomes oxidized when it gains oxygen atoms and/or loses electrons in the process and becomes reduced when it gains electrons (or loses oxygen atoms and/or gains hydrogen atoms). A compound that loses electrons must give them to another compound or atom. Oxidation-Reduction:

- takes place between pairs of atoms or compounds
- is ongoing,
- takes place in stages

Lower redox potential in wine (a "reductive state") can lead to Volatile Sulfur Compounds and stinky wine. The higher the redox potential, the better the hold on the oxygen.

Typical Redox Compounds Found in Wine and Their Redox Potentials*

Half-Reaction	Redox Potential (Volts) @ pH 3.5
$\frac{1}{2}O_2 + H^+ + 2e^- \rightarrow H_2O$	1.02
$Fe^{3+} + e^- \rightarrow Fe^{2+}$	0.77
$O_2 + 2H^+ + 2e^- \rightarrow H_2O_2$	0.48
Dehydroascorbate $+ 2H^+ + 2e^- \rightarrow$ Ascorbate	0.27
$Cu^{2+} + e^- \rightarrow Cu^+$	0.16
Oxaloacetate $+ 2H^+ + 2e^- \rightarrow$ malate	0.10
Acetaldehyde $+ 2H^+ + 2e^- \rightarrow$ ethanol	0.04
(Glutathione-S)2 $+ 2H^+ + 2e^- \rightarrow$ 2Glutathione-SH	−0.023
$SO_4^{2-} + 4H^+ + 2e^- \rightarrow SO_2 + 2H_2O$	−0.24
*Reformatted from Zoecklein, et al., 1995.	

Compounds change their attributes when they become oxidized, especially those in wine. The conversion of alcohol to acetaldehyde and further to acetic acid is such a process. Unfortunately, it can be a difficult process to reverse.

Thiols or Sulfur Flavors

Sulfur is one of the top 10 elements in our bodies, on earth and in the universe. Most extracted sulfur is used to make sulfuric acid (H_2SO_4), which is also produced by the combination of rain and SO_2 from coal burning or volcanic eruptions. (Some sulfuric acid results from wine making.) The gas—SO_2—will be discussed in detail later. The following pages discuss sulfur's organic compounds.

Over 100 organic volatile sulfur compounds (VSCs) have been identified in wine. Some of them are quite "smelly" and considered faults in wine. Others are less so, but most sulfur compounds will mask true fruit flavors in wine. This is the result of oxygen deprivation—sulfur compounds in a reductive environment.

How to Deal with VSC Problems

Sulfur is both a necessity for and a byproduct of fermentation. It usually appears in the form of Hydrogen sulfide (H_2S) which increases when the yeast cell is nitrogen-starved and continues exuding a product that it cannot use.

Normally, a yeast cell absorbs sulfites and sulfates to produce the nitrogen-based (and also sulfur-containing) amino acids cysteine and methionine (see diagram to the right). But when the nitrogen runs out, the cell can no longer use the sulfur that it has converted to H_2S and secretes it.

In a "reductive" environment—low redox potential—the H_2S will persist, and may even become a more complex sulfur compound, such as mercaptan, or a disulfide. In an "oxidative" environment (high redox potential, with abundant oxygen atoms) the sulfurs will often precipitate out as elemental sulfur

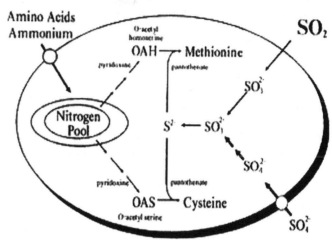

Sulfide Production During Fermentation

From Vladimir Jiranek : Australian & New Zealand Grapegrower and Winemaker

$$2H_2S + O_2 \leftrightarrow 2H_2O + 2S$$

or they can become sulfur compounds with higher perception thresholds.

Redox potential is related to pH: high pH favors low redox potential and a reductive environment. A low pH favors a high redox potential and an oxidative environment.

A high H_2S level toward the end of fermentation can be eliminated by oxidizing the must through "splash racking," but should not be done long after fermentation. If mercaptans are detected and not hydrogen sulfides, adding O_2 may only make the problem worse, turning mercaptans to dimercaptans and other VSCs.

VSCs can be divided into "heavy" sulfur compounds (bigger molecules that boil above 90°C) and "light" sulfur compounds (which boil under 90°C). H_2S is a "light" sulfur compound and, therefore, can be more easily eliminated. Luckily for wine drinkers, the heavier VSCs have higher perception thresholds. Although they are often present, they are not detectable because they are in concentrations below that threshold. Unluckily, some high-threshold compounds can reduce to lower-threshold compounds when oxygen is very low (see the following page). Early screw tops allowed this to happen in the bottle. When VSCs are detected before bottling, it is necessary to lower their concentration below the OAV level.

To get rid of light and heavy VSCs, follow the direction on the following pages. The methods usually involve copper and ascorbic acid. Remember, however, that you may want to keep some VSCs, such as

- 4-mercapto-4-methylpentan-2-one (grapefruit)
- benzenemethanethiol (smoky/gunflint)

So go easy on the copper!

Examples of Sulfur-like Off Odor Compounds in Wines

SLO	Sensory Description	Sensory Threshold (ug/L)	Boiling Point (°C)
Hydrogen Sulfide	Rotten egg	0.5	–61
Carbonyl Sulfide	Ether	3.0	–50
Methyl Mercaptan, Methanethiol	Stagnant water	1.5	6
Ethanethiol	Onion	1.1	35
Dimethyl Sulfide	Quince, truffle	10.0	35
Methionol	Cooked cabbage	1200	90
Diethyl Sulfide	Ether	0.9	92
Dimethyl Disulfide	Quince, asparagus	15.0	109
Diethyl Disulfide	Garlic, rubber	4.3	151
Thioesters			

Light / Heavy

The two Methanethiol (also called mercaptan) molecules below each lose a hydrogen to oxygen which becomes water.

$$2 \quad \text{H}_3\text{C}-\text{SH} \quad \xrightarrow{\text{oxidation}} \quad \text{H}_3\text{C}-\text{S}-\text{S}-\text{CH}_3$$

methanethiol ←── reduction ── dimethyl disulfide
sensory threshold 0.2 ppb   sensory threshold 12 ppb

$$+ \quad = \quad + \quad \text{H}_2\text{O}$$

Causes and Cures of VSCs

Hydrogen sulfide (H$_2$S)

Hydrogen sulfide usually produces the odor of rotten eggs. Its sensory threshold is 1 ppb. It can mute fruit odors even when it is not recognized as H$_2$S. Sulfur is an essential element in yeast metabolism, and yeast can produce H$_2$S by the reduction of elemental sulfur, by catabolism of the amino acid cysteine and by the reduction of inorganic sulfur, such as residues from fungicide sprays.

If H$_2$S is noted at the very beginning of the fermentation, it is usually a result of elemental sulfur sprays. The cure is to let the must cold-settle and rack it off the sediments (which will contain much of the sulfur). Then restart fermentation.

Some yeasts produce more H$_2$S than others (*Montrachet* often causes reduction). Stressed yeast cells will tend to cause H$_2$S later in the fermentation, especially if there is insufficient available nitrogen in the must for them to reproduce and metabolize sugars. Additions of diammonium phosphate with vitamins at the beginning and half way through fermentation helps avoid H$_2$S production by the yeast.

The Cure: The earlier the winemaker detects H$_2$S, the easier it is to get rid of. To check for H$_2$S, add a couple drops of copper sulfate to a glass of the must or wine and swirl. If the fruit odor comes back, or the egg odor lessens, the wine contains H$_2$S.

If the problem is merely muted fruit odors or just the slightest egg smell, aerating (slightly oxidizing) the wine will usually take away the annoying bouquet. This is often the best course if the wine has just finished fermentation, and especially if fermentation is still continuing and H$_2$S has developed.

Rack the wine off the gross lees (precipitated dead yeast cells) first. Do not over oxidize. Especially do not oxidize the wine if you smell any mercaptans, which have a garlicky, cabbage or rubber smell. Oxidizing will produce dimercaptans, which are harder to purge from your wine.

Mercaptans

Sometimes called thiols (although that is a larger class) mercaptans smell like cabbage, burnt rubber, garlic and, in the worst cases, sewer gas. Do not aerate.

The Cure: Copper Sulfate. However, copper sulfate won't remove mercaptans once they've become dimercaptans, which first need to be "re-oxidized" with the addition of ascorbic acid. Raise SO$_2$ to the level recommended for the pH of the wine. Add 30 ppm of 1% ascorbic acid to the must or wine (11.25 ml/gal) just in case some of the mercaptans have become dimercaptans. Wait a few days and add .3 ppm of 1% copper sulfate solution to the wine (.45 ml/gal). Stir vigorously. Let this sit for a day or two.

If mercaptans and H$_2$S persist, repeat. (You can also do bench trials in the beginning to determine how much copper is necessary.) You will need to get the copper out of your wine—.5 ppm is the maximum allowed by law. Copper can add a metallic taste and cause haze in wine. Add yeast hulls to the wine, stirring vigorously, and rack off the hulls as soon as the wine has settled. Repeat the fining-racking process one or two more times. If you have doubts, send a sample to a lab for metal analysis.

Dimethyl Sulfide

This is the most abundant biological sulfur compound found in the atmosphere (mostly as a result of phytoplankton emissions). It has a distinct vegetal smell, often of corn.

The Cure: Same as for mercaptans.

Other Volatile Sulfurs Found in Wine

Some of the volatile sulfur compounds in wine (adapted from Jamie Goode http://www.wineanorak.com/nsinwine.httm)

Compound	Sensory impact	Notes
Hydrogen sulfide (H_2S)	Rotten eggs, swamp gas	The earliest and most common VSC found in wine, usually occurring at the end of fermentation because of stressed yeast. It most often gives a rotten egg odor.
Mercaptans (also called thiols)	A large group of very smelly sulfur compounds. The two following are the most common.	Hydrogen sulfide if left in the wine will devolve into mercaptans. This is a big worry for winemakers.
Ethyl mercaptan (ethanethiol)	Raw onion, earthy, burnt match	Generally a negative odor except in very small concentrations and combined with other strong odors.
Methyl mercaptan (methanethiol)	Rotten and cooked cabbage, burnt rubber, stagnant water and halitosis.	One of the compounds implicated in screwcap reduction
Dimethyl sulfide	Quince, truffle at low levels; cooked corn and vegetal at high levels.	A "light" VSC (Boiling point, like H_2S, is below 90°C).
Diethyl sulfide	Rubber	
Carbon disulfide	Sweet, ethereal, slightly green.	
Dimethyl disulfide	Quince, asparagus at low levels; vegetal when high.	
Diethyl disulfide	Garlic, burnt rubber	
4-mercapto-4-methylpentan-2-one (4MMP) 3-mercaptohexan-1-ol (3MH), 3-mercaptohexyl acetate (3MHA)	Tropical fruit/passion fruit at low levels; cat's urine when levels are out of hand.	Common in *Sauvignon Blanc* but also found in red wines where they can contribute to the blackcurrant fruit aroma.
Benzenemethanethiol	Smoky/gunflint	Identified in boxwood. It is common in *Sauvignon Blanc, Chardonnay & Semillon*.
Methionyl acetate	Mushroom/ string bean	Found in *Cabernet Sauvignon*.

The "Other" Sulfur: SO$_2$

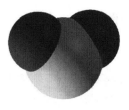

Potassium metabisulfite, often referred to as just "meta," is often added to wine in order to inhibit microbes and oxidation. It becomes Sulfur Dioxide (SO$_2$) when added to wine. For general purposes, it will be helpful to remember the following facts:

- Almost all of the effective part of "meta" becomes two products, molecular SO$_2$ (molecular sulfite) and HSO$_3$ (bisulfite). Of these, molecular SO$_2$ is hundreds of times more effective than HSO$_3$. Also, only molecular SO$_2$ is effective at killing wild yeast and bacteria. It is small enough to enter the cell and disrupt enzyme activity.
- The lower the pH, the higher the percentage of molecular SO$_2$. (At pH 3.0, 7% is molecular SO$_2$. At pH 4.0 that drops to 1%.)
- Bisulfite HSO$_3$ can bind with other chemicals in wine—sugars, acetaldehyde, and phenolic compounds—to become bound SO$_2$. The remaining free SO$_2$ (molecular sulfite and bisulfite) continues to be effective at destroying microbes and preventing oxidation. But the HSO$_3$ and the SO$_2$ are in their same ratios (related to pH) so the more free SO$_2$ that becomes bound the less molecular SO$_2$ the wines will have available to kill microbes.
- Total SO$_2$ = free SO$_2$ + bound SO$_2$. (Free SO$_2$ and bound SO$_2$ are measured in mg/l or parts-per-million of the wine.)
- When free SO$_2$ binds with anthocyanins, they become colorless because it binds with acetaldehydes and eliminates a bridge in the tannin-anthocyanin complex. For that reason one should be cautious in adding SO$_2$ during red wine fermentation.
- Free SO$_2$ prevents oxidation in white wines by binding with the precursors and products of oxidation.
- Since free SO$_2$ kills bacteria, it should be used sparingly (<10 ppm) until after malolactic fermentation (MLF) is over.
- Maintaining free SO$_2$ is difficult in unstable or sweet wines, where sometimes 80–90% of the SO$_2$ in the additions of "meta" to the wine become bound SO$_2$ within a few days.
- The optimal level of free SO$_2$ is 20–40 ppm to maintain .8 ppm molecular SO$_2$ between pH 3.0–3.5.

Sulfur Dioxide to a Fault

Free SO$_2$ smells like matchsticks and can burn the nose above 100 ppm free. It is often noticeable at 60 ppm in white wine and, if noticeable, is graded as a flaw in wine judging. At above 150 ppm free SO$_2$, the wine becomes undrinkable.

The Cure: If you have too much free SO$_2$ you can loose some of it by splash racking. As the free SO$_2$ comes out of solution (vaporizes) more bound SO$_2$ will sometimes take its place lowering the total SO_2 even if the free SO_2 does not change much. But this type of oxidation of SO_2 is not a perfect solution: it must be done in a gentle way to keep the ethanol from forming Acetaldehyde. A better choice is placing wine in neutral oak for six months where it can reduce free SO_2 by up to 60 ppm. Some winemakers resort to Hydrogen peroxide (H_2O_2) which is effective at binding with the free SO_2, but that creates sulfuric acid. Additions of H_2O_2 are illegal in some countries and states.

Volatile Acidity as a Fault

Volatile Acidity includes all the acids that can enter a gaseous phase at room temperature. These are *not* the fixed acids that "give backbone" to a wine (malic acid, tartaric acid and citric acid). Fixed acids, TA and pH are discussed in the previous sections.

The most common volatile acid in wine is acetic acid (vinegar), but VA also includes ethyl acetate, an ester, and other unpleasant smelling products (fumaric, propionic and butyric acids). VA makes up a very small portion of any wine. (Even most vinegars contain only 5% acetic acid.) The development of a small amount of VA quickly becomes evident. Most people can detect acetic acid at 700 mg/l (or .07%) about one-eighth the concentration of most wines' fixed acids. Above that point, it is often considered a fault.

Causes of Acetic Acid

Numerous microbes produce VA in wine, the most important being the following:

- *Acetobacter* and *Gluconobactor,* which are aerobic ("oxygen requiring") bacteria.
- Lactic Acid Bacteria (LAB), although some varieties more than others.
- Wild yeast strains, such as *Kloeckera apiculata, Pechia membranaefaciens* and, to a lesser degree, some strains of *Saccharomyces cerevisae.*
- *Pediococcus* bacteria, which are anaerobic and, therefore, a concern after bottling.
- *Botrytis*, which is found on damaged fruit, usually as a result of *Acetobacter,* which is carried in by fruit flies and bees.
- *Brettanomyces* and its *telemorph Dekkera* cause acetic acid in the presence of oxygen.

Factors affecting VA

It is important to remember that the higher the pH during alcohol fermentation and during malolactic fermentation (MLF), the greater the acetic acid production.

VA is also a natural product of all wine fermentations, but usually in negligible, non-detectable amounts.

Causes of Ethyl Acetate

This compound, which smells like fingernail polish remover, is rarely produced during MLF but is a byproduct of yeast fermentation. It is more commonly a derivative of alcohol and acetic acid combined, as can be seen in the following diagram:

Formation of an Ester (Ethyl Acetate) from a carboxylic Acid (Acetic Acid) and an Alcohol (Ethyl Alcohol or Ethanol)

Monash Scientific Glass Blowing Services +61 3 9791 4442

Avoiding VA

It is interesting to note that the British Columbia Amateur Wine Makers Association blames the winemaker for all the ethyl acetate, but for only 80% of the acetic acid found in wine. (Both are almost always the fault of decisions made during the winemaking process.) VA must be closely monitored, especially when the must has a high pH (3.6 or higher). SO_2 levels must be kept high to avoid microbial spoilage associated with VA. This is an almost impossible quandary if the winemaker wishes to have the wine go through malolactic fermentation (MLF).

SO_2 levels must be low for the wine to successfully go through MLF. The only safe option is to raise the acidity, thereby lowering the pH. Malolactic fermentation is safest at pH levels between 3.2 and 3.5. At those levels *Oenococcus oeni* is favored over other "problem-causing" Lactic Acid Bacteria (Costello et al 1983). Also, the cleaner the fruit, the lower the microbial spoilage levels will be during fermentation. The limited use of SO_2 before fermentation to kill off wild yeast and detrimental bacteria is also advisable. (Most of it will be used up during fermentation and therefore not be in solution to affect MLF.) For control of MLF see Ben Rotter 2003–2009 and Henick-Kling.

The options are limited for the winemaker who has made a high-VA wine. There are companies that will visit a winery and remove the VA through cross-flow filtration and an anion exchange resin, but that costs $2 per gallon or more and requires a minimum of several thousand gallons of wine. One can attempt to restart the fermentation by adding fresh yeast and sugar, in which case some of the VA will "blow off," but it is difficult to obtain a vigorous fermentation on a finished wine, and the alcohol levels may become prohibitive. The best option is not to let the horse out of the barn in the first place.

- Start with clean fruit and sanitary equipment.
- Protect non-fermenting juice and finished wine with SO_2.
- Always monitor the pH and VA during fermentation.
- Monitor SO_2 levels in finished wine and keep wine topped up in container.
- Acidify or blend musts and wines to keep the pH in safe limits.

Things to Avoid...

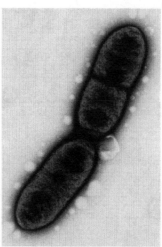

Acetobacter Mary Parker Institute of
Food Research, Norwich

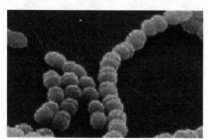

Lactic Acid Bacteria

Gluconobacter oxydans
Heather Owens University
of Wisconsin

How to Avoid Them

Level of free SO_2 that will kill most LAB

Free SO_2 needed for	
0.8 ppm molecular SO_2	
pH	Free SO_2
3	14
3.1	18
3.2	22
3.3	28
3.4	35
3.5	44
3.6	55
3.7	69
3.8	87
3.9	109

Malolactic Fermentation (MLF) and Lactic Acid Bacteria (LAB)

Malolactic fermentation is the conversion of malic acid (the "harsher tasting" of a wine's two principal acids) to lactic acid (a fairly soft acid that is associated with "rounder tasting" wines). Although the process varies according to the substrate and strain of LAB it follows this reaction:

Malic acid (L-) → Lactic acid + Carbon dioxide
$COOH\text{-}H_2OC\text{-}H_2C\text{-}COOH \rightarrow CH_3\text{-}CHOH\text{-}COOH + CO_2$

For every gram of malic acid metabolized, about .67 grams of lactic acid are produced (and the rest, .33 grams, becomes CO_2). However, most LAB can convert some sugar to lactic acid, and the worst of them effectively metabolize tartaric acid and glycerol to acetic acid. It is important to remember that not *all* malic acid in a wine is transformed to lactic acid—only malic (L−). Commercially available malic acid contains both malic (D+), which is non-convertible, and malic (L−).

MLF Effects on Wine

Malolactic fermentation (MLF) will result in a flaw in a wine *only* under certain conditions:

- when it takes away from the normal quality of a varietal wine (the floral, fruit-driven characteristics of Rieslings, Gewürztraminer, Vidal, etc.),

- when its byproduct, diacetyl (the butter flavor you get when you buy "movie popcorn") negatively affects the varietal characteristic of a wine.
- when its causal agent metabolizes tartaric acid, pentose and glycerol and creates excessive volatile acidity.
- when it takes place in still wines after bottling (especially if there is residual sugar).

For most red wines it is better to allow them to proceed through MLF, especially if sterile filtration is not part of the process, to avoid a "sparkling" red wine resulting from MLF after bottling. (While many wine drinkers enjoy this light effervescence it is considered a flaw by judges.) Likewise, because most forms of LAB will compete with yeast to convert sugar to acetic acid and other products, it is fortunate that MLF usually occurs after yeast fermentation has ended (Lafon-Lafoucade 1983). For this reason, modern red vinification usually involves inoculating the almost-finished must or fresh wine with a safe MLF bacteria—one with a high success rate and low VA production.

Diacetyl in Wine

The metabolic pathway for the production of diacetyl is fairly well understood. (See the figure to the right.) It starts with the breakdown of citric acid into oxaloacetic acid and continues to the final product, 2,3-butanediol, creating various byproducts along the way. For *Oenococcus oeni* this takes place after the completion of malic acid conversion to lactic acid (Dharmadhikari 2002). However, because several varieties of LAB can produce diacetyl, and the environment—pH, available oxygen, alcohol, temperature— also affects its production, the amount of diacetyl that will be found in a

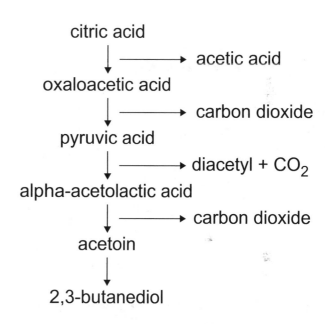

finished wine is difficult to predict. In addition, the diacetyl that is produced can also be reabsorbed through metabolic activity of both LAB and yeast.

Controling Diacetyl

People differ in opinion as to how much diacetyl is acceptable or beneficial to wine. For white wines 2–3 mg/l is thought to favorably enhance the flavor, especially in Chardonnay. It seems that 4–5 mg/l does not reduce the quality of red wine. Threshold levels vary according to grape variety with diacetyl being detectable in Chardonnay at .2 mg/L while requiring 14 times more to be detectable in Cabernet Sauvignon (Martineau et al 1995).

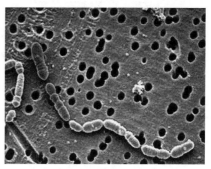

Oenococcus oeni

A number of parameters can be controlled to limit or increase diacetyl. The greater the amount of oxygen in a wine going through MLF the more diacetyl will be produced. Also diacetyl production is greatest after (L–) malic acid has been metabolized, so it is important to monitor the acids in the wine (e.g. using paper chromatography) from the end of alcoholic fermentation onward. When the wine is most sensually acceptable, MLF should be stopped by sterile filtration and/or SO_2. Keep in mind that SO_2 will bind with the diacetyl, making it less obvious. But as the bound SO_2 becomes free through time, most of the diacetyl will again become detectable.

The Good, the LAB and the Ugly

Lactic Acid Bacteria come in various species and varieties. As mentioned on the previous pages, *Oenococcus oeni* is the one most favored by winemakers. But caveat emptor, for there are many sub-species, including wild versions that produce high amounts of acetic acid. Usually the winemaker can count on the larger commercial producers for consistency in the bacteria that they sell to winemakers.

LAB is classified as homofermentative and heterofermentative (fermentations producing single or multiple end products respectively), according to the substrates it metabolizes, the resulting products, and the pH at which it is most productive. The following table, from Ben Rotter's web site "Improved Winemaking," represent a few of these species of LAB. The genera *Pediococcus* and *Lactobacillus* will be dealt with in more depth later.

Homofermentant

Pediococcus cerevisiae	
Pediococcus damnosus	mainly present in musts and at high pH after malolactic fermentation
Pediococcus pentosaceus	sometimes present lower populations
Pediococcus parvulus	
Lactobacillus casei	sometimes present lower populations
Lactobacillus plantarum	mainly present in musts
Streptobacterium	

Heterofermentant

Leuconostoc gracile	
Oenococcus oeni	most resistant to low pH
Leuconostoc mesenteroides	sometimes present lower populations
Lactobacillus hilgardii	
Lactobacillus fructivorans	
Lactobacillus desidiosus	
Lactobacillus hilgardi	sometimes present lower populations
Lactobacillus brevis	sometimes present lower populations

Other Microbes that Create Faults

Brettanomyces

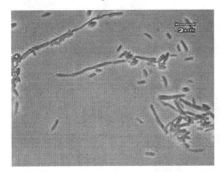

If there is a mousy, horsey, sweaty, wet dog, leathery, stale hamburger, barnyard character in the wine, here's the irony: some tasters like it (in small quantities, of course!). It is caused by *Brettanomyces*, one of six strains of the *Dekkera* genus of yeast (a "bad brother" of *Saccharomyces*). At its worst, it produces mousy, metallic odors and lots of acetic acid. In small amounts, the "barnyard and saddle leather" (4-ethylphenol) or "bacon, cloves and smoke" (4-ethylguaiacol) characteristics may add complexity to the wine.

4-Ethyl-guaiacol (4EG) = Smoky-spicy
4-Ethyl-phenol (4EP) = Stables, horsey, sweaty-saddles
The ratio of 4EG to 4EP can lead to negative odors!
4EG+4EP can = 4-*Vinyl-phenol* = Band-Aid (sticking plaster)

Other Aromatic Products of Brettanomyces

- *Isovaleric acid* = goat, rancid
- *Ethyl decanoate* = plastic
- *Trans-2-nonenal* = burning tires
- *Isoamyl alcohol* = fruity

Brettanomyces Needs the Following:

- Sugar (carbons from): glucose, fructose, cellulose, trehalose or ethanol
- Nitrogen: amino acids
- Oxygen: low levels desirable
- Temperature: 13°C–30°C
- Free SO_2 (<30 mg/l)
- Time: weeks to years; It can live up to 35 years in some cases
  (adapted from Henick-Kling, 2010).

Removal and Cure

- Avoidance is best: Keep cellar and equipment clean. Avoid damaged fruit.
- Keep pH low (preferably under 3.5).
- Use sufficient SO_2.
- To guarantee elimination: Filter at .8 µm or finer absolute membrane
  (Ibid and Umiker 2010).

Zygosaccharomyces bailii

This is one of a genus of common food yeasts that seem difficult to kill or eliminate on winery equipment. *Zygo-saccharomyces bailii* can withstand some SO_2 as well as flourish in high-sugar environments. This makes them a danger to unfiltered sweet wines. They can withstand heat as high as 37°C. They create white granule deposits in white and rosé wines and create water and acetic acid. They seem to be primarily anaerobic.

***Zygosaccharomyces bailii* Mary Parker**
Institute of Food Research, Norwich

Candida stellata

Candida is an early yeast genus that lives in botrytized grapes, and the species C. *stellata* seems to continue until the end of fermentation, contributing both positive flavors (apricots and honey) as well as the flavors of sauerkraut and ethyl acetate. There is some question as to its contribution to the botyrytis taste in wine, but though it is considered a spoilage organism, many feel it contributes to the wine complexity (Henschke 2000).

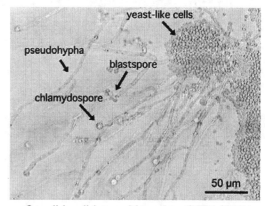

Candida albicans: Y tambe, GFDL/GNU

Mycoderma vini or "Flowers of Wine"

This refers to a category of microbes that grow on the surface of wine—both the yeast *Candida mycoderma* and possibly several forms of bacteria. They all seem to need oxygen and produce water, CO_2 and acetaldehyde and are sensitive to SO_2.

"Ropiness"

Credited to long silky chains of bacteria, including *Streptococcus mucilaginous*, *Leuconostoc sp.*, varieties of *Lactobacillus* and most commonly *Pediococcus parvulus* (also a vigorous producer of ethyl acetate). These produce a fibrillar polymer called β-glucan, which creates a thick oily structure. Although anaerobic, these bacteria are sensitive to SO_2.

Lactic Souring

If there is residual sugar at the end of fermentation, lactic acid bacteria may attack grape sugars. The glucose is converted into lactic acid and acetic acid, and the fructose can be converted into a nasty material called *mannitol*, imparting a "sweet and sour" taste.

"Mousiness"

This unpleasant (as described) aroma is usually the result of a species of Lactic Acid Bacteria. Pediococcus spp. is the most common, but it is also caused by strains of *Leuconostoc mesenteroides* and some strains of the recommended *Oenococcus oeni*. It involves the oxidation products

Lysine + ethanol → Acetyl tetrahydropyridines

The compounds responsible for smell are two 2-acetyl tetrahydropyridine isomers (2-acetyl-1-pyrroline), at a very low sensory threshold around 1.6 ppt (Henick-Kling 2010).

Amertume, Tourne and Graisse

These terms all describe changes in wine caused by Lactic Acid Bacteria.

- **Amertume** describes the "bitterness" that results when LAB attacks glycerin turning it to acetic acid.
- **Tourne** (to "turn to brown") occurs when *Lactobacillus brevis* converts glucose and fructose to acetic acid (Bibek 2003). Peynaud and Spencer (1984) attribute tourne to the total fermentation of a wine's tartaric acid to vinegar by the same organism.
- **Graisse** ("greasy" or "oily") is an older description of the effects of ropiness in wine.

Geranium Smells

This fault is usually the result of malolactic bacteria's effect on sorbate. Sorbate is a great yeast production inhibitor—but that is all it does. With MLB it can produce 2,3 ethoxy, 3,4 hexadiene, most often associated with geraniums. If you choose to use it in sweet wines to insure that the residual sugar does not referment in the bottle (secondary fermentation) then you *must* also include a good dose of SO_2 to kill off the MLB.

Butteriness, Buterscotch and Rancid Butter

These are three worsening levels related to diacetyl (2,3 butanedione), a by-product of MLB. In Chadonnays, the butteriness is sometime a positive attribute; in red wine, more often a fault. It is often a result of MLB working on citric acid after exhausting all the malic available. Never acidify with citric acid if MLB is expected.

Atypical Aging (ATA) and other Indefinables

The wine chemistry world is not sure what causes ATA, but it may have figured out how to cure it. Although the condition is associated with rapid loss of soundness in the wine, in some cases (especially in Germany) it has been implicated in a "taint" that smells like wet towel, wax, dirty dish rag and naphthalene (mothballs).

ATA is also associated with certain white varieties that produce wine that is sometimes surprisingly short–lived. This has often been a problem with Seyval Blanc, a hybrid grown in much of the eastern USA. The wine will generally become flat and lose its fruit starting one year after bottling—something similar to the effects of acetaldehyde production, but without oxygen. The substance 2-aminoacetophenone, which relates to the metabolism of the amino acid tryptophan and is more commonly found in American native varieties and their crossings, seems to be conducive to ATA development (Schneider, 2010). However, the greatest correlation found was with low nitrogen levels in the fruit at veraison. Water stress might be implicated in the process (Zoecklein, 2003).

The cure: Avoid water stress in the vineyard and monitor nitrogen levels. If the winemaker has experienced ATA in past wines, or suspects it may occur in wines she is making, then additions of 150 mg/liter of ascorbic acid to the wine after the final racking—but months before bottling—are necessary.

Geosmin

Wines thought to have this quality are often a product of *Atinobacteria* or *Ascomycetous* fungi—most often *Penicillium* in conjunction with *Botrytis cinerea* (La Guerche et al 2005). They leave a distinctive earthy, musty and even turnip odor—so geosmin is sometimes confused with an effect of terroir. The smell may also contribute to what is perceived as cork taint.

Lightstrike

Wine exposed to sunlight or light of 325–450 nm, unless bottled in ultraviolet-resistant glass, may change its nature and develop negative odors. Red wines rarely suffer lightstrike because their phenolic compounds better protect them. The odors are often described as wet cardboard and wet wool. Even white wine in green glass will be affected after only 31 hours of fluorescent light. But wine in flint (clear) bottles needs only 3.3 hours for the same degradation (Dozon, 1989).

Chemical Interactions and Biogenic Amines

Amines are nitrogen-containing bases that are produced by yeast and other micro-organisms in must and wine. They are found in variable concentrations in most, if not all, fermented foods (cheese, wine, yogurt, fermented meat, etc.).

There are two concerns:

- Some biogenic amines have physiological effects on susceptible individuals. Most common are headaches and other allergic reactions—often credited to SO_2—caused by histamines (Medina, 1999).
- Cadaverine (you can guess the etymology) and putrescine create odors of decaying flesh. In high concentrations (>100 mg/l) can cause wines to smell "metallic, meaty or putrid."

Causes: Amino acid precursors are enzymatically changed in various microbes. Most common culprits are *Lactobacillus, Pediococcus*, and wild strains of *Oenoccocus*. Some strains of *Saccharomyces* and *Dekkera* cause biogenic amines.

Bad News: Biogenic amines might be detectable in most red wines going through MLF (Marcobal, 2005). This is especially true in the presence of residual sugars.

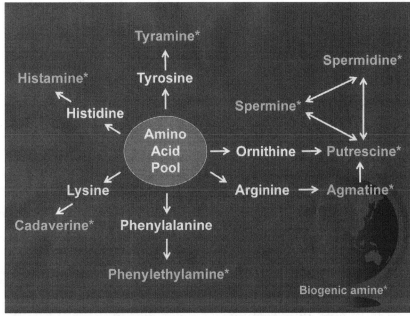

Both insets Adapted from Edwards (2010) and

Good News: Most wines are generally below concentration levels thought to cause problems (Edwards, 2010; Marcobal, 2005). In addition, new yeast and *Oenococcus* strains have been developed for their low biogenic amine production (see van Vuuren n.d. for discussion). At right are the results of recent testing for biogenic amines (ETS labs, 2009; Edwards, 2005).

Suggestion: In addition to aldehydes, the above are better blamed for headache and discomfort than is SO_2 (which can eliminate the producers of biogenic amines).

B. Total of 295 wines (CA, OR, and WA)*

1. Putrescine <1 to 296 mg/L (84 wines ≥10 mg/L).
2. Cadaverine <1 to 4 mg/L
3. Histamine <1 to 72 mg/L (52 wines ≥10 mg/L).
4. Tyramine <1 to 20 mg/L (11 wines ≥11 mg/L).
5. Highest total amine in a wine → 359 mg/L
6. WA wines only
   a. Total of 29 samples
      (3 wines >25 mg/L total biogenic amines)

*ETS Laboratories (2009)

Effects of Tannins on Taste

Condensed tannins represent the most common phenolic compounds found in grapes (mostly in their seeds and skin). They are primary contributors to taste and mouth feel. These polymers include

- catechin—found mostly in the seeds
- epicatechin—found mostly in seeds

- epigallocatechin—only found in the skin
- epicatechin gallate—found in skin and seed

In addition to offering health benefits to humans, assisting in color retention and promoting longevity of the wine, tannins affect primary taste attributes that define many red wines (Harbertson *et al* 2008). These are not the ellagitannins and vanillin phenolics found in oak. Tannin's most pronounced sensory effect is astringency.

It is probably not correct to classify a high level of tannin as a fault, but it sometimes acts as such. Harbertson (ibid.) has demonstrated more than a 30-fold difference in tannin content of red wines, which suggests that in some wines the tannins so dominate other flavors as to mask them permanently (a criticism of the best of the1975 Bordeaux vintage even today). A colloquial classification of the effects of tannin, used by wine critics:

soft (good)	hard (not good)
round (good)	young (not good)
mature (good)	persistent (not good)

While it is thought that "young" and "hard" tannins are associated with seed tannins (especially "green seeds"—see the section on berry readiness) there is not yet any taxonomy of tannin effects. What is known is that tannins will combine with other anthocyanins to fix color, and *possibly* "mellow" or round out the astringency. Acid and sugar levels also affect tannin perception. Tannins usually precipitate out of the wine with time (or gelatin fining) lessening their effect.

Is there a Petroleum Crisis (...in Riesling)?

The most common aroma associated with Riesling wine is not one of its many monoterpenes, alpha (*lily of the valley*), hotrienol (*lime tree*), linalool (*rose*) but the closely related C13 norisoprenoid compound 1,1,6-Trimethyldihydronaphthalene (TDN). However, this distinctly kerosene-smelling constituent does not exist in the grape before it becomes wine. Therein lies the problem.

It has been determined that carotenoids in the grape—*yes, keep those carrots out of the vineyard!!*—interact with sunlight to create the precursors to TDN in the wine. Hydrolysis during winemaking, storage, and later acid-catalyzed rearrangements bring to most Rieslings some of that petrol flavor. The two variables for this terpene-like compound are sunlight and time in the bottle (Sacks et al 2010). The must of very warm sunny vintages will not taste of petrol at the end of fermentation but will develop those flavors later (see graph at right).

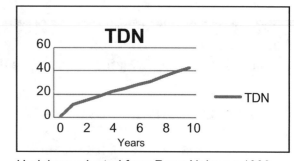

Hudelson adapted from Rapp Nahrung 1998

Even though the OAV for TDN is quite high it is thought by many to be the discriminating factor in identifying a Riesling. While Germans have come to value that petroleum aroma, many Americans and especially Australian wine judges seem to think that too much of it is a flaw. Don't like it? Drink early!

Glossary

2-phenylethanol—An alcohol with a pleasant floral (rose) odor.

2,3 ethoxy, 3,4 hexadiene—The geranium smell usually resulting from MLF in wine containing sorbate.

4-ethylguaiacol—Caused by Brettanomyces and having a "bacon, cloves and smoke" odor.

4-ethylphenol—Caused by Brettanomyces and having a "barnyard and saddle leather".

4-mercapto-4-methylpentan-2-one (4MMP)—A thiol (VSC) that odor is Tropical fruit/ passion fruit at low levels; cat's urine at higher levels.

Acetaldehyde—CH_3CHO The most important aldehyde in wine, and the toxic substance into which ethanol is converted in your liver.

Acetaldehyde dehydrogenase—a group of enzymes that help convert acetaldehyde into acetate in the liver.

Acetic acid—CH_3COOH A simple carboxylic acid that gives vinegar its smell and sourness. Produced in wine by various bacterial infections.

Acetobacter—A genus of aerobic bacteria that is (too) common in wine musts and changes ethanol to acetic acid.

Adaptation (sensory)—(also Neural Adaptation) is a change in responsiveness of a sensory system (such as olfactory or taste) to stimulus, usually due to long-term persistent stimulation of the nerves.

Afferent nerve—The means by which impulses are carried from sense receptors to the central nervous system.

Alcohol dehydrogenase (ADH)—A group of seven liver enzymes that are catalysts for converting alcohol to acetaldehyde.

Alcohols—An organic compound in which the (–OH) hydroxyl group is bound to a carbon atom: ethanol, methanol, isopropyl etc.)

Aldehyde—An organic compound with a carbonyl (O=C) at the end of the molecule (**ketones**, have carbonyl in the center). Often fragrant.

Amino acids—Molecules containing nitrogen that are the building blocks of proteins, the basis of all life forms.

Anaerobic—"Not requiring oxygen"

Antabuse—(also Disulfiram) In prescription form, a drug that blocks the production of acetaldehyde dehydrogenase and causing sickness.

Anthocyanins—Any of many water-soluble red to violet plant pigments related to the flavonoids,

Antioxidant—Molecules that inhibit the oxidation of other molecules. They inhibit the production of free radicals that damage cellular tissue.

Apical—The apex, or farthest out in a plant or structure.

Arabinose—A pentose (5-carbon) sugar.

Aribitol—A **Polyol**.

Astringency—A drawing, puckering, tactile sensation caused by grape and oak tannins that are an essential part of wine flavor.

Atypical Aging—A flaw more commonly found in wine made from interspecific hybrid resulting in rapid fruit loss and off smells (wet towel, mothballs) thought to be caused by 2-Aminoacetophenone and possibly stressed grapes.

Bacteria—The most basic (and maybe most numerous) organisms in the tree of life. One of a number of organisms found in wine that affect its taste.

Bentonite—A natural fining agent for wine made of fine clay (usually, Montmorillonite).

Benzenemethanethiol—A volatile thiol causing smokey/gunflint odors found in wine. Also found in boxwood.

Benzene ring—The beautiful hexagon ring C_6H_6 with three double-bonds between carbons. Their most common representation in wine are the phenolics and tannins.

Benzyl alcohol—An aromatic alcohol with a benzene ring. When oxidized (via botrytis) becomes benzylaldehyde imparting bitter almond taste.

Bisphenol A (BPA)—A phased-out phenol used to make polycarbonate plastics and known to be estrogenic.

Bisulfite—HSO_3 The less effective of two sulfur ions (representing 93–99%) resulting from metabisulfite added to wine.

Botrytis cineria—A necrotrophic fungus that grows on grapes which in the right conditions raises sugar (lowers water content) and in humid conditions, can ruin a crop with sour off-flavors.

Brettanomyces—Asexual forms of the Dekkera genus of yeast, that are slow but persistent and contribute a variety of (both good and bad) odors to wine.

Cadaverine—A biogenic amine found in urine, seamen and (needless to say) putrefying animals…Oh, and did I say, sometimes in wine?

Candida—A genus of yeast found in the hunan body. In wine Candida stellata continues to grow through unchecked fermentations, sometimes contributing fruity (apricot/honey) but more often sour tastes to the wine.

Cane—On a grape vine, last year's shoot (new growth) which has hardened to wood, producing new shoots at nodes. A form of pruning as opposed to "spur pruning."

Carbonation—Carbon dioxide gas dissolved in wine from byproducts of yeast fermentation, bacterial fermentation or sparging with CO_2 gas.

Carboxyl group—A ("functional") group of atoms attached to other molecules that will always react in the same way. The carboxyl includes a carbon with a double bond to oxygen (**carbonyl**) and an O-H (**hydroxyl**).

Carboxylic acids—Acids characterized by having one or more carboxyls (see above). They are protein (H) donors. Acetic acid is an example.

Carotenoids—What has 40 carbons and absorbs the color blue? Breakdown of carotenoids is implicated in the production of **β-Damascenone** and, more topical, TDN.

Casse—A haze caused by insoluble metal salts; iron and copper are the most common causes.

Catabolism—The process by which cells breakdown polymers into smaller units (monomers) and create (anabolism) new molecules and/or energy.

Catechin—A polyphenol (flavonoid, subgroup flavan-3-ols), found mostly in the seeds of grapes.

Chemical Contaminants—Anything not natural to grapes, fermenting must or wine.

Chroma—The perceived intensity of a specific color relative to other colors in a photograph.

Chromatographic paper—A simple (OK, it requires formalin) means by which amounts of tartaric, malic and lactic acid can be measured in wine.

Circumvallate papillae—Eight to twelve structures on the dorsal (top) side of the tongue that function to remove material from that region by flushing saliva around the tongue.

Citric acid—One of the lesser fixed acids found in wine. Unfortunately sometimes used to acidulate wine.

Citronellol—A monoterpene (Terpenoid alcohol) found in many flowery wines with the odor of citronella.

Concentration—How much of a substance is mixed with another, in percentage to parts-per-trillion.

Cordon—The "arms" of a grapevine spur-pruned (not cane pruned).

Corked wine—The old sofa, wet cardboard, wet washcloth smell caused by tyrene or TCA.

Cross-flow filtration anion exchange resin—In wine, filter system in which the permeate (water, alcohol, acetic acid) can be eliminated. In the case of wine with high VA, the permeate is pumped through a + charged resin and returned to the wine.

Cysteine—An amino acid, that when catabolized during fermentation by yeast can cause H_2S.

Damascenone—A rose ketone found in found in both red wine (berry odors) and white wine (floral odors).

Dekkera—Genus of yeast causing several strains of Brettanomyces; usually considered a spoilage organism.

Delphinidin-3-glucoside—(also Malvidin)An anthocyanin that contributes some of the red to wine, also, a possible natural control of insulin production for humans.

Damascenone—A rose ketone found in found in both red wine (berry odors) and white wine (floral odors).

Dekkera—Genus of yeast causing several strains of Brettanomyces; usually considered a spoilage organism.

Diammonium phosphate (DAP)—A water soluble ammonium phosphate salt that is used to supplement YAN in grapes.

Diatomaceous earth—(Also called kieselgur) Naturally occurring crumbly siliceous rock that is used as a filter medium for wine (and swimming pools).

Diethyl disulfide—A heavy Volatile Sulfur Compound that smells of garlic and burnt rubber.

Diethylene glycol (DEG)—A toxic solvent that can impart a sweet taste if added to food or wine.

Dimercaptan—What you get if you oxidize wine with high levels of mercaptans. Don't!

Dimethyl disulfide—A VSO developing from mercaptans that smells of quince and asparagus.

Double salt method—Using calcium carbonate to lower acid in wine without raising pH drastically. Acidex

Egg whites—Used as a gentle fining agentin wine.

Ellagitannins—Tannins contributed by oak which interact with oxygen and acetaldehyde to help stabilize crimson in red wines.

Elemental sulfur—The crystalline sulfur or sulfate/sulfite minerals found in nature. Used as a fungicide on grapes.

Enzymes—Proteins that act as catalysts in chemical reactions, latching onto molecules and breaking them apart, or reassembling new molecules.

Epicatechin—A cis configuration of catechin, found mostly in grape seeds (also found in cacao seeds).

Epigallocatechin—A polyphenol (flavonoid, subgroup flavan-3-ols) only found in the skin and thought to have health benefits.

Epoxy resin—A copolymer (made up of two chemicals) that is used with fiber glass. Popular for fermentation tanks, but may impart taint.

Erythritol—One of many non-fermentable sugars found in wine. It has 60–70% sweetness of sucrose and is non-caloric.

Esters—Chemicals formed when alcohols and acids condense; they are often fragrant.

Ethyl-4-phenol—The barnyard/saddle smell that results from Brettanomyces breakdown of sugar and amino acids.

Ethyl Acetate—In wine, the result of acetic acid and ethanol resulting in a fingernail polish remover odor.

Ethyl butanolate—An ester occurring in wine that is often described as the odor of pineapple.

Ethyl decanoate and Ethyl hexanoate—two important esters found in chardonnay and thought to be scalped by plastic (bottles, fermenters, closures).

Exteroceptive—Relates to a sense organ, although it can be just a receptor on the tongue, that receives stimuli from outside the body.

Filiform papilla—One of the four types of lingual papillae, this one not sensing taste but movement.

Fining agent—One of many adjuncts added to wine to help it clarify, either by charge, agglutination or enzymes.

Fixed acids—In wine, the non-volatile acids such as malic, tartaric, succinic and citric acids. (Sometimes confusingly called organic acids.)

Flavanoids—One of two types of polyphenols ("phenolics") found in wine; this type includes anthocyanins, Flavanols (Flavan-3-ols or tannin building blocks) and Flavonols which are glycosides.

"Floral" wines—A general reference to wines with flowery and light fruit (peach, pineapple, lychee, etc.) fragrance: Rieslings, Gewurtztraminers and Muscats are most commonly associated with this colloquial expression.

Foliate papilla—Taste buds at the sides and base of the tongue.

Fungiform papilla—Mushroom shaped taste buds that cover most of the tongue and sense the five tastes.

Furfural—An aromatic aldehyde (sweet, almond, bread) contributed to wine usually by oak aging.

Fusarium—One of the genera of organisms implicated in the conversion of chlorine to TCA (corked wine).

Fusel alcohols—(also called Fusel Oils) Higher alcohols (more than two carbons) which include propanols, butanols, amyl alcohol, and although not an alcohol, furfural is often included in the group. They are common in the "tails" of distillation, whence the German name for "bad liquor."

Gelatin—A positively charged (in most wines) fining agent made of animal collagen (bones and skin).

Geosmin—(literally "earth smell") An earthy, musty (turnip?) smell in wine resulting from ascomycetous fungi in conjunction with Botrytis cineria.

Gluconobactor oxydans—A species of the genus Acetobacter that is common in wine and creates vinegar out of alcohol and oxygen.

Glutathione—A tripeptide (containing three amino acids) that assists (along with the enzyme acetaldehyde dehydrogenase) in reducing acetaldehyde to an acetate. Glutathione contributes the amino acid cysteine to the process.

Glycerol—(also glycerin/glycerine) after ethnanol and water, the most abundant substance in wine. A viscous (alcohol-like) polyol that is thought to give mouth feel and a sweetness to wines (although there is no evidence for this) glycerol's qualities are varied, forming the backbone of triglycerides, a substitute for ethylene glycol and the basis of nitroglycerine.

Gout de terroir—"Taste of the earth" is a reflection of the different tastes wines of same variety of grape give when grown in different locations.

G protein-coupled receptors—Receptors in the tongue that signal to a nerve when bitter, sweet or savory is tasted.

H_2S—Hydrogen Sulfide is the most common VSC in wine. It smells like rotten egg at a very low threshold, and at 1PPB can mute the flavor of a wine. It is quite reactive and if left in the wine will contribute to Mercaptans, or Disulfides.

HDPE—High-density polyethylene is a strong plastic (higher specific strength than LDPE) that is chemical resistant, withstands high heat and allows some oxygen transfer with time. For these reasons it is used in wine making.

Hangtime—The amount of (extra) time grapes are left on the vine past normal (24 Brix) sugar accumulation (Nick Dokoozlian–Napa Valley Grape Growers–2004 symposium). This is thought to add different (better?) flavors to the wine that is produced.

Heavy sulfur compounds—Sulfur compounds (like Dimethyl Disulfide) that boil at or above 90°C.

Heterocyclic compounds—Most comonly a benzene ring with at least one non-carbon element and at least one carbon (usually 4–5). But it can be a ring with three to eight atoms that are not all the same.

Histamine—A nitrogen compound that acts as a neurotransmitter causing an inflammatory response to foreign stimuli.

Hydrogen ion—A Hydrogen atom with more than one electron (anion) or less than one electron (cation). Most important in acid-base reactions.

IBMP—(3-isobutyl-2-methoxypyrazine) The pyrazine associated with "Green Bell Pepper" odor. In slight amounts, not a fault.

Idiocentric—"caused by the person" or related to the person.

Inversion—referring in this case to invert sugar and the process (through heat or enzymes) of separating the disaccharide sucrose into two monosaccharides, fructose and glucose.

Ion channels—Taste receptors on the tongue that sense sour and saltiness.

Isinglass—A fining agent made from the airbladder of fish.

Isoamyl Alcohol—A higher alcohol (boiling point 131°C). See fusel alcohols.

Isoamyl acetate—Formed from the above and acetic acid, it has a fruity, banana odor.

Isobutyl alcohol—See fusel alcohols.

Isovaleric acid—(also 3-Methylbutanoic acid) can be the product of Brettanomyces, smells like goat, rancid cheese and is a component of foot odor.

Kloeckera apiculata—A naturally occurring yeast found on grapes that ferments sugars at temperatures lower than saccharomyces cerevasie but dies off when alcohol reaches about 6%. It also produces high quantities of acetic acid.

LDPE—Low density polyethylene.

Laccase enzyme—Enters the grape with Botrytis Cineria infections and can cause problems, especially in red wine, during fermentation, causing red pigments to brown.

Lactic Acid Bacteria LAB—A family of bacteria that changes malic acid to lactic acid, but can also produce acetic acid, diacetyl and other products.

Lactic acid—A "milder" tasting acid than malic or tartaric acid.

Lactones—A 1960s rock group... No, the result of esterification (see esters) in the grape or during fermentation. Some may be associated with certain grape varieties (similar in function to terpines). Others result from aging in wood: like the coconut odor of the *cis* isomer of β-methyl-γ-octolactone.

Limbic system—(also called the Paleomammalian brain) It supports various functions, one which is olfaction, but also closely associated with memory and emotion.

Linalool—A terpenoid alcohol associated with Muscat and other flowery wines.

MALB Multicolored Asian Lady Beetle—(*Harmonia axyridis*) similar to the American "Lady Bug" was introduced to the Americas to control aphids.

Malic acid—The harsher of the two major acids found in grape wine. (L-) Malic represents about one-half of the acid that can be converted to the "milder" Lactic acid.

Malolactic Fermentation MLF—The microbial process of converting Malic acid to Lactic Acid and CO_2.

Manitol—A sugar alcohol (Polyol) that is a byproduct of MLF, especially if fructose was present. Contributes a viscous, sweet and irritating finish.

Mechanoreceptors—Mechanical stimuli receptors that sense touch, pressure, streaching and motion. As many as $100/cm^2$ on the tongue.

Mercaptans—Thiols resulting from reactions of H_2S with alcohols or amino acids sulfurs. A few are pleasant smelling, but most are faults and are more difficult to eliminate from wine than H_2S.

Methyl mercaptan (Methanethiol) and ethyl mercaptan (Ethanethiol)—Two of the more common thiol faults: methyl-generally smells like swamp water and ethyl-like onions.

Metabolites—The products and intermediate products of metabolism (cellular catabolism and respiration).

Metallic haze—(See Casse)

Methanol—Methyl Alcohol, CH_3OH, the simplest of alcohols; poisonous, and a very minor product of grape fermentation.

Methoxypyrazine—A class of pyrazines usually having vegetable qualities (see IBMP).

Micro-organisms—An organism too small to be seen without a microscope.

Microbe—See Microorgamism.

Mitral cell—Neurons located in the olfactory bulb.

Molecular sulfite—(SO_2) That sulfur which is most effective as an antimicrobial agent in wine; its percentage in total sulfites is higher at a low pH.

Monoterpenes—Organic molecules found in wine that usually impart pleasant odors (see **Linaloo** and **Citronellol**).

Mouth feel—The effect of wine on the mechanoreceptors of the mouth.

Mucus membrane—For our purpose, the endodermal lining of the mouth (including tongue) and nasal cavity where mucus is secreted.

Nalgene bottles—A trademark of Nalge Nunc International, originally most of the bottles were made of polycarbonate resin thermoplastic which used the estrogenic **BPA**.

Nasal receptor cell—Olfactory receptor cells protruding from the ofactory bulb into the nasal cavity that receive certain volatile molecules (conceptually, as in receiving the single piece missing from a jigsaw puzzle) and send a signal to the olfactory sensory neuron.

Neo-cortex—The top layer of the cerebral hemispheres where memory (especially of odors) is stored and higher mental functions occur.

Nitrogen compounds—Amines, most important for grapes and wine are the amino nitrogens (ammonia derived) that are necessary for yeast metabolism (fermentation) and those found in pyrazine compounds.

Norisoprenoid—Formed from the cleavage of carotenoids and associated with **TDN** some classify this as a terpene.

Odor—The result of volatilized chemical compounds fitting into nasal receptor cells and stimulating the limbic system.

Odorant—Volatilized chemical compounds.

Oenococcus oeni—The preferred **LAB** species because of low acetic acid production.

Olfactory bulb—A multi cellular, multi-layered structure in the top of the nasal cavity that receives stimuli from the millions of olfactory receptor neurons filtering them through the intermediation of the Glomeruli and forwarding signals to the brain. There is a suggestion bidirectionality in the circuit – both sides of the snyapses are dendrites that can release neurotransmitters – allowing the brain to regulate sensitivity and discrimination of odors.

Organic acids—In wine, they are the fixed acids (as opposed to the volatile acids like acetic acid). Because both fixed and volatile acids have carbons and are "organic," a better term is "fixed acids."

Organoleptic—Dealing with sensory analysis of wine through taste, smell and sight.

Oxaloacetic acid—In MLF it acts as an intermediate in the production of diacetyle. An intermediate in the citric Krebs cycle[1] and gluconeogenesis.

PET—(Polyethylene terephthalate) is a hard thermoformed polyester plastic used for wine bottles in some countries. Differing from the ubiquitous PET soft drink bottle, wine bottles must be lined with an O_2 barrier to keep the wine from becoming oxidized.

pH—Think of it as the "power of the Hydrogen ion" in wine. (It is actually an *approximation* of the negative logarithmic scale of a molar concentration of Hydronium ions (H_3O^+).) Most important for winemaking is, while **TA** measures the concentration of acid in a wine, pH measures the "activity" or power of those acids. That power helps to keep wine sound. The lower the pH the higher the concentration of Hydronium ions. On pH's 0-14 scale, water and blood at 7.0 are neutral. Wine, which runs from pH 4.0-3.0 is 1,000 to 10,000 times more acidic than water. Got that? The measurement of pH in soils is a different topic.

PP—(Polypropylene) A thermoplastic that is not used much for fermentation or wine products (possibly grape lugs).

PVPP (Polyvinylpolypyrrolidone)—The cross linked version—Crospovidone—is used as a non-soluble fining agent that links to phenolic compounds that cause browning in white wine. It also "softens" red wine by removing tannins.

Pichia membranaefaciens—A wild yeast found on grapes that can produce high levels of acetic acid.

Pediococcus—A very common genus of LAB that tends to produce high acetic acid. Also associated with "mousiness."

Penicillium—A common fruit mold, associated with *Botrytis cineria*, and yes, the production of the the antibiotic penicillin.

Phenols—A class of chemicals related to esters and alcohol (a hydroxyl group—OH) that bond to aromatic hydrocarbons. In wine they form the polyphenols (flavanoids, non-flavanoids, tannins etc.) and oak imparted eugenol, guaiacol and gallic acid.

Polyol—Higher alcohols (boil at *higher* temperature than ethanol) sometimes called sugar alcohols. See Glycerin.

Polyphenols—Large molecules generally produced in the grape's skin, stems and seeds. Also includes oak derivatives.

Potassium metabisulfite—The most common form for additions of SO_2 to must and wine. Commonly called "meta" it produces between. One gram of meta will render about .57 gms of SO_2 but the powder loses its potency quickly in storage.

Propanol—A byproduct of fermentation, although, unless yeast is stressed, only in very small quantities. Rubbing alcohol.

Putrescine—A biogenic amine that, similar to cadaverine, is produced by the breakdown of amino acids during fermentation. Can contribute foul odors of decay and rot to the wine in large quantities. Toxic levels for putrescine have not been established.

Pyrazines—In wine, refers to a class of heterocylic aromatic compounds (see **methoxy-pyrazines** and **IBMP**).

Pyruvate acid—A common byproduct of fermentation, production determined by yeast strain and must pH. An intermediate in the production of diacetyl.

Redox—The process of reduction/oxidation that is constantly taking place in wine. Reduction is the loss of oxygen atoms (the gaining of hydrogen atoms and electrons. Oxidation is the gaining of oxygen atoms and the loss of electrons and or hydrogen atoms.

Redox potential—The potential of the wine to hold its oxygen atoms. Low redox potential allows for reduced sulfur compounds to develop. Redox potential is greatly affected by the pH of the wine. High pH will lower the redox potential.

Reduced Sulphur Compounds—Smelly thiols resulting from low redox potential and the byproducts of fermentation.

Resveratrol— (3,5,4'-trihydroxy-trans-stilbene) A non-flavanoid polyphenol found in the grape skin that is shown to be an enormous health benefit if we could just drink enough red wine (about 80 ltrs./day?).

Retro-nasal—The backflow from the esophagus after swallowing of a wine's odors into the nose. Usually different from the nasal induced odor.

Rhamnose—A non-fermental pentose sugar.

Ropiness—Generally non-salubrious wine, usually with some stringy yeast formation floating in the solution.

Saccharomyces cerevisae—("sugar loving yeast") The species of sac yeast that is responsible for almost all commercially made wine and beer.

Sapa—Grape juice boiled down to one-third its content and used to sweeten wine in early Rome. **Defrutum** was the juice reduced by 50%. Because the Romans preferred using lead pots to boil the juice (the lead seemed to sweeten it more) the suffered from Saturine gout.

Saprophytic organisms

Saturation of color—How one sees a color by variable brightness. As an example, red in very low light appears the same a gray.

Saturnine gout—Lead poisoning from wine enhanced with Sapa or Defrutum. The disease seemed to fit the character of the planet.

Scalping—The chemical process of taking away odors (pleasant and repulsive) and often associated with fining of wine or storage in certain plastics.

Secondary fermentation—Referencing both alcohol fermentation in the bottle (as with sparkling wines in methode champagnoise) and MLF.

Secondary metabolites—Products of cell metabolism that are not essential to cell growth and reproductivity. Anthocyanins are an example.

Sediment in wine—Precipitation ("coming out of solution as a solid") of one or more of a wine's constituents such as tartrate crystals, or heavy tannins.

Settling juice or wine—Allowing non-soluble solids to precipitate and fall to the bottom of the solution.

Silicon dioxide—"Kieselsol" is used as a colloidal fining agent. It can be manufactured with either charge.

Sorbate—Potassium Sorbate is a food preservative that in wine is effective at inhibiting saccharomyces yeasts but not effective at killing bacteria. It should always be used in sweet wine with SO_2 to avoid the geranium odor derived from MLF action on Sorbate. Some people claim it creates a bubblegum flavor if over used in sweet wine (http://www.bcawa.ca/winemaking/flaws.htm).

Sorbitol—A sugar alcohol that is minor in wine, but sometimes added to wine illegally (Burda and Collins 1991).

Spermidine—One of the secondary biogenic amines found in wine. While beneficial claims have been made for spermidine—reducing aging in some organisms (by autophagy)—it can also react with nitrous acids and its salts in wine forming nitrosoamines which are carcinogenic (Santos 1996).

Spinning cones—A machine that takes alcohol out of wine using centrifugal force.

Sterile filtration—Conceptually, removing all organisms from the wine.

Succinic acid—A minor acid in wine derived from fermentation. It is said to add a bitter/salt taste to wines, but is probably more important for its production of esters in wine.

Sulfur Dioxide SO$_2$—Used in wine as an antimicrobial/antioxidant agent. It binds with aldehydes and other constituents making wine more "stable." As one of the sulfites its effectiveness is greater at a lower pH. See **molecular sulfite**.

Sulfur compounds—Organic compounds with sulfur that tend to be unpleasantly odiferous. These include thiols and sulfides.

Sulfites (bound and free)—SO$_2$ and HSO$_3$, called bisulfite, will bind to sugar, acetaldehyde, anthocyanins etc, becoming "bound sulfites." In that state SO$_2$ is no longer effectual in destroying micro organisms or scavenging oxygen. Therefore, it is important to know how much free sulfur is in the wine at different points in its life (after years in the bottle, there rarely is any free SO$_2$ left).

Sulfuric acid (H$_2$SO$_4$)—A result of hydrogen peroxide and SO$_2$ in wine. Used as a standard in the measurement of TA in France. While very illegal, sulfuric acid has been added to wine in order to lower pH without increasing TA at the rate that other acids would.

Synthetic pesticides—A non-natural pesticide, created through biochemistry. "Natural" (not always "organic") are found the in natural world, like the fungicides sulphur and copper. Most synthetic pesticides target the "pest" and disrupt some part of its life cycle.

TDN 1,1,6- Trimethyldihydronaphtalene—C13 norisoprenoid—The "petrol" (kerosene) smell associated with Riesling. It accumulates in bottle aging of good Rieslings. Considered a fault most places.

THQ level—Target Hazard Quotients were developed by the U.S. Environmental Protection Agency to determine safe limit values of pollutants for long-term exposure to top soils at waste sites. The scale has also been used to determine the long-term health risk of eating fish containing heavy metals. Naughton and Petroczi (2008) applied the scale to wines. That the scale is a "dimensionless index of risk" (ibid.) and assumes continued exposure (ie: drinking the same metal-contaminated wine every day for the rest of your life) lessens its realistic value for wine fault studies.

TCA (Tyrene)—2,4,6 trichloro anisole is the product of a number of molds that interact with chlorine cleaners. See corked wine.

TTB—Alcohol and Tobacco Tax and Trade Bureau is an arm of the US Treasury and regulates all alcohol production and sales in the United States. Unfortunately, as a guardian for quality and purity, its personal – and some would argue the products it oversees—are over-taxed.

Taint—Generally, a contaminant or pollutant found in food or drink, usually in very small (but not necessarily harmless) quantities.

Tannin—A polyphenol that imparts astringency to wine. They are reactive with proteins and various other organic compounds including amino alkaloids and amino acids.

Tartaric acid—One of the two major fixed acids in wine (the other being malic acid).

Taste receptor cell—See **G protein-coupled receptors** and **Ion Channels**.

Terpenes and Terpenoids—A very aromatic class of hydrocarbons (derived from isoprenes) responsible for many of the odors we associate with Riesling, Gewurztraminer, Muscat and other flowery wines. When a terpene's carbon chain is modified or oxidized, it is called a terpenoid (see Linalool and Norisoprenoid).

Thermo-afferent receptors—Thermorecptors on the tongue that are sensitive to heat and cold are found in numerous forms including nociceptors which sense painful heat.

Thioesters—Odorless sulfur-compounds (esterified carboxylic acid with a Thiol attached) that can go through hydrolysis and form smelly sulfur compounds.

Thiol—Basically, a large number of compounds that contain a sulfur-hydrogen bond (the correlate of alcohol's O-H). Often called mercaptans.

Trans-2-nonenal—A product of the Brettanomyces yeast, the aroma often described as "burning tires."

Tribromoanisole TBA—Similar to TCA but involving the biomethylation of bromides found in the winery to produce a "corked" odor.

Trichoderma longibrachiatum—Along with Penicillium one of the genera of molds that might cause **TCA** and **TBA**.

Vanillin—A nonflavonoid phenol in wine derived from oak aging.

Vinyls—Derived from Latin for wine. An organic compound containing a vinyl group ($-CH=CH_2$). Most commonly associated with polyvinyl chloride (PVC).

Viscosity—The "thickness" of a liquid. The more viscous a wine, the more syrupy it appears in the glass.

Volatile—For our purposes, compounds that evaporate at normal temperature and pressure.

Volatile Acidity VA—In wine, mostly acetic acid and sometimes small amounts of ethyl acetate which, if detected, are considered faults.

Xylose—One of many pentose sugars found in wine.

YAN (Yeast Available/Assimilable Nitrogen)—The amino nitrogen supplied by grapes and used by yeast in fermentation. If enough does not exist, add it!

Yeast—A single-celled, eukaryotic micro-organism that is part of the fungi kingdom. The wine producing version is **Saccharomyces cerevisae**.

Volatile sulfur compound (VSC)—Those thiols and sulfides that cause odors in wine. 1 ppt that's *one part-per-ten-trillion*, or .1ng./L. = 1/1,000,000th

Bibliography

Al Nasir, R., A.G. Jiries, M.I. Batarseh, F. Besse. *Pesticides and trace metals residue in grape and home made wine in Jordan,* **Enviromental Monitoring and Assessment**. 2004.

Bibek, Ray. **Fundamental Food Microbiology**. Third Edition, CRC, 2003.

Belancic, Andrea[1] and Eduardo Agosin. *Methoxypyrazines in Grapes and Wines of Vitis vinifera* cv. Carmenere, **American Journal of Enology and Viticulture**. 58:4:462–469, 2007.

Burda, K. and M. Collins. J-food-prot. Des Moines, Iowa: International Association of Milk, Food and Environmental Sanitarians. May 1991. v. 54(5) p. 381–382.

P. Cabras; E. Conte, *Pesticide residues in grapes and wine in Italy,* **Food Additives and Contaminants**. v.18, n.10, Oct. 2001.

Cannavan, Tom. "Aromas and Flavors" in Tom Cannavan's wine-pages.com

Collings, V.B. *Human taste response as a function of location of stimulation on the tongue and soft palate,* Percep. **Psychophys**. 16:169–74, 1974.

Costello, P.J., Morrison, R.H., Lee, R.H., and Fleet, G.H. (1983). Numbers and species of lactic acid bacteria in wines during vinification. Food Technol. Aust. 35, 14–18.

Cox, R.J.; R.R. Eintenmiller; J.J. Powers. "Mineral Content of Some California Wines" in **Food Science** Vol. 42:3, 2006.

Dharmadhikari, Murli. Some Issues in Malolactic Fermentation Acid Reduction and Flavor Modification, **Vineyard and Vintage View**, Volume 17(4), p. 4–11, 2002.

Dozon, N.M. and A.C. Noble. "Sensory Study of the Effect of Fluorescent Light on a Sparkling Wine And Its Base Wine." **AJEV** Vol. 40, No. 4, 1989.

Dworkin, Martin, ed. **The Prokaryotes:a handbook on the biology of bacteria**. Springer, 2006.

Edwards. C.G. Biogenic amines. Presented at the Washington Association of Wine Grape Growers annual meeting, Kennewick, WA. February 3–5 (2010).

Eggers, Nigel. The Odor and Aroma of Wine. https://people.ok.ubc.ca/neggers/Chem422A/The%20Odor%20and%20Aroma%20of%20Wine.pdf

Firestein, Stuart. "How the olfactory system makes sense of scents." **Nature** 413, 211–218 (13 September 2001).

Fox, Stuart, "Report Claims Less Than 1 Percent of Corks Are Noticeably Tainted." Wine Spectator, August 20, 2009.

Franson, Paul. *New Filters Remove TCA from Wine,* **Wines and Vines**. May 22, 2008.

Fugelsang, K.C. *Zygosaccharomyces, A Spoilage Yeast Isolated from Wine.* **CATI**, 1996.

Fugelsang, K.C. and Charles G. Edwards. **Wine microbiology: practical applications and procedures**. 2nd ed. Springer, 2007.

Shiban Ganju. "Three Quarks Daily." http://www.3quarksdaily.com/3quarksdaily/2008/09/the-smells-of-d.html

Gibson, George and Miklos Farkas. "An Article for Competition Wine Judges and of Interest to Competitors." BCAWA web site.

Harbertson, James F.[1], Ryan E. Hodgins[2], Lisa N. Thurston[2], Larry J. Schaffer[2], Matthew S. Reid[2], Josie L. Landon[3], Carolyn F. Ross[3] and Douglas O. Adams. Varieability of Tannin Concentrations in Red Wine, **AJEV** 59:2:210–214, 2008.

Hartmann, Peter J. **The Effect of Wine Matrix Ingredients on 3-Alkyl-2-methoxypyra-zines Measurements by Headspace Solid-Phase Microextraction (HS-SPME)**. Ph.D. Thesis, Virginia Polytechnic Institute, 2003.

Hein, K.A. 2005. **Perception of vegetative and fruity aromas in red wine and evaluation of a descriptive analysis panel using across product vs. across attribute serving**. M.S. thesis, University of California, Davis.

Henick-Kling, T. Control of malo-lactic fermentation in wine: Energetics, flavour modification and methods of starter culture preparation. **J. Appl. Bacteriol.** Symp. Suppl. 79, 29S–37S 1995.

Hennick-Kling, Thomas. "Mousiness, Brettanomyces and Cork Taint," presentation at the Washington Association of Wine Grape Growers annual meeting, Kennewick, 2010.

Henschke, Paul A., A. Soden, H. Oakey, Leigh Francis. *Effects of co-fermentation with Candida stellata and Saccharomyces cerevisiae on the aroma and composition of Chardonnay wine*, **Australian journal of grape and wine research**. ISSN 1322-7130, Vol. 6, No. 1, 2000, pp. 21–30.

Huang, Angela L., Xiaoke Chen, Mark A. Hoon, Jayaram Chandrashekar, Wei Guo, Dimitri Tränkner, Nicholas J. P. Ryba and Charles S. Zuker. **Nature**. 42, 934–938, Aug. 24, 2006.

Jackson, Ronald S. **Wine Tasting: A Professional Handbook**. Academic Press, 2002.

Jackson, Ronald S. **Wine Science: Principles and Applications**, 3rd ed. Academic Press. 2008.

Johnson, Hugh and Jancis Robinson. **The World Atlas of Wine** (sixth edition) Beazley, 2007.

Kennedy, James. "Understanding Grape Berry Development" in Practical Winery and Vineyard Magazine, July/August 2002.

Lafon-Lafoucade, S., A. Lonvaud-Funel and E. Carre. *"Lactic Acid of Wines: Stimulation of growth and Malolactic Fermentation"* in **Antonie van Leeuwenhoek**. 49:3, Springer, 1983.

La Guerche, S., Chamont, S., Blancard, D., Dubourdieu, D., Darriet, P. "Origin of (-)-geosmin on grapes: on the complementary action of two fungi, botrytis cinerea and penicillium expansum." in **Antonie Van Leeuwenhoek**. 2005 Aug; 88(2):131–9.

Lesschaeve, Isabelle **Sensory Evaluation of Wine and Commercial Realities: Review of Current Practices and Perspectives**. Am. J. Enol. Vitic., Jun 2007; 58: 252–258.

Liu, S.Q. and G.J. Pilone. 2000. An overview of formation and roles of acetaldehyde in winemaking with emphasis on microbiological implications. **International J. of Food Science and Technology**. 35: 49–61.

A. Marcobal, M.C. Polo, P.J. Martín-Álvarez and M.V. Moreno-Arribas. Biogenic amine content of red Spanish wines: comparison of a direct ELISA and an HPLC method for the determination of histamine in wines." **Food Research International**. Volume 38, Issue 4, May 2005, Pages 387–394.

Martineau, B., Acree, T.E. and Henick-Kling, T. Effect of wine type on threshold for diacetyl. **Food Research International**. 28(2), 1995.

McGee, Harold. "For a Taster Wine the Next Trick Involves…" **New York Times,** Jan. 13, 2009.

Medina, M.A., A.R. Quesada, I.N. de Castro and F. Sanchez-Jimenez. 1999. Histamine, polyamines and cancer. **Biochem. Pharmacol**. 57, 1341–1344.

Mumma, Amy, Anne Johansen, Holly Pinkart, John Hudelson, Sara Rybka, Celia Braun Faiola, Brad Snaza. Wine Quality Initiative, CWU 2009.

Naughton, D.P. and Petroczi, A. **Chemistry Central Journal**. Vol. 2, Oct. 29, 2008.

News.yahoo.com Nigeria child deaths from tainted syrup rise to 84

Nielsen, J.C., and Marianne Richelieu. Control of flavor development in wine during and after malolactic fermentation by *Oenococcus oeni*. Applied and Environmental Microbiology. 65(2): 740–745, 1999.

Nriagu, Jerome O. *Saturnine Gout amoung Roman Aristocrats*, **New England Journal of Medicine**. 660-3, March, 1985.

Pan-Europe: http://www.pan-europe.info/Media/PR/080326_notes.pdf

Peynaud, Emil and Alan Spencer. **Knowing and Making Wine**. 1984.

Pohl, P. *What do metals tell us about wine?* **Trends Anal Chem**. 26: 941–949, 2007.

Proust, Marcel. **In Search of Lost Time** (Vol. 1) Modern Library, New York, 1992 (1919).

B.C. Rankine. *Formation of higher alcohols by wine yeasts, and relationship to taste thresholds,* **Australian Wine Research Institute**, Adelaide, S. Australia, 1967.

Rapp, A. **Nahrung/Food** Volume 42, Issue 06, Pages 351–363 Verlag GmbH, Weinheim, Fed. Rep. of Germany.

Rotter, Ben. http://www.brsquared.org/wine/ "Improved Winemaking, www.brsquared.org/wine" (2002–2009).

Sacks, Gavin. Bound for Trouble: The Life and Death of Riesling Flavor Precoursers in the Vineyard ("Dude, You're Bound for Trouble:" Life in detox with Riesling aroma precursors.) WAWGG 2010 Annual Meeting.

Sacks, Gavin, Justine Vanden Heuvel, Alan Lakso, Imelda Ryona, Bruce Pan and Justin Scheiner. "Vegginess in the Wine or the Winemaker." WAWGG 2010 Annual Meeting.

Sacks, Gavin; Justine Vanden Heuvel; Terry Acree; Jim Meyers; Misha Kwasniesski, "Dude, You're Bound for Trouble: Life in Detox with Riesling Aroma Percursers." paper presented at WAWGG 2010 Annual Meeting.

Sajilata, M.G.K. Savitha, R.S. Singhal, and V.R. Kanetkar. "Scalping of Flavors in Packaged Foods." http://www.net-lanna.info/Food/Articles/11020049.pdf

Santos, M.H.S. 1996. Biogenic amines: Their importance in foods. **Int. J. Food Microbiol**. 29: 213–231.

Schneider, "Volker. Primer on Atypical Aging" in Wines and Vines, No. 4, 2010, 45–51, 2010.

Segurel, M.A., A.J. Razungles, C. Rous, M. Salles, and R.L. Baumes. 2004. Contributions of dimethyl sulfide to the aroma of Syrah and Grenache noir wines and estimation of its potential in grapes of these varieties. **J. Agric. Food Chem**. 52: 7084–7093.

Stockert, Christine M. and David R. Smart. **Proceedings of the 2nd Annual National Viticulture Research Conference**, University of California, Davis, July 9–11, 2008.

Umiker, Nicole L. Management of Dekkera (Brettanomyces) by SO_2 and Filtration" paper presented at International Cool Climate Symposium, ASEV annual meeting, 2010.

van Vuuren, Hennie J. J. Malolactic yeast ML01 – The Facts at http://www.landfood.ubc.ca/wine/vanvuuren/vanvuuren_malolatic-yeast.html (n.d.)

Vivas, Nicolas and Yves Glories. "Role of Oak Wook Ellagitannins in the Oxidation Process of Red Wine Aging in **Am. J. Enol. Vitic**. 47:1:103–107 (1996).

Walker,[†]Teresa, Justin Morris, Renee Threlfall,[‡] and Gary Main. pH Modification of Cynthiana Wine Using Cationic Exchange in **J. Agric. Food Chem**., 2002, 50 (22), pp. 6346–6352.

Webb, A. Dinsmoor and Richard E. Kepner The Separation of Desirable High-Boiling Components from Fusel Oil in **Am. J. Enol. Vitic**., Dec 1956; 7: 126–130.

Wencker, D., B. Spiess, P. Laugel. *Influence of hexacyanoferrate (II) based treatments upon the elimination of heavy metal traces in wine. II. The case of cadmium,* **Food Additives & Contaminants: Part A**, Volume 7, Issue 3, PAGES 375–379, May, 1990.

Zoecklein, Bruce. **Enology Notes** #77. July 21, 2003.

INDEX

Understanding Wine Technology, 3rd Edition

David Bird

Foreword by Hugh Johnson

Any student who's ever logged credits in a viticulture and enology class knows Bird's book. It's the most widely assigned wine-science primer in the English speaking world. This completely revised and updated edition to Bird's classic textbook deciphers all the new scientific advances that have cropped up in the last several years, and conveys them in his typically clear and plainspoken style that renders even the densest subject matter freshman-friendly. Paperback, 6 x 8 inches, 328pp., full-color illustrations and charts, fully indexed.

$49.95 ISBN: 978-1-934259-60-3

Concepts in Wine Chemistry, 2nd Edition

Yair Margalit

The primary text for scores of universities and hundreds of winemakers in a dozen countries, Concepts in Wine Chemistry, by physical chemist and winemaker Yair Margalit, details the basic and advanced chemistry behind the practical concepts of winemaking: must and wine composition, fermentation, phenolic compounds, aroma and flavor, oxidation and wine aging, oak products, sulfur dioxide, cellar processes and wine faults. Dr. Margalit also gives the biochemist's slant on the contentious question: is wine good for you? Paperback, 7 x 10 inches, 446pp., illustrated, charts and graphs, fully indexed.

$89.95 ISBN: 978-1-934259-48-1

Concepts in Wine Technology

Yair Margalit

This detailed how-to guide, by physical chemist and winemaker Yair Margalit, is organized in the sequence of winemaking: in the vineyard – proper maturation, soil and climate, bunch health, vineyard disease states and grape varieties; pre-harvest – vineyard management and preparing the winery for harvest; harvesting – destemming, crushing and skin contact as it applies to both red and white grapes to pressing, must correction and temperature control; and finally fermentation and cellar operations. Paperback, 7 x 10 inches, 263pp, illustrated, charts, graphs, index.

$39.95 ISBN: 978-1-934259-46-7

Winery Technology & Operations

Yair Margalit

The predecessor to Dr. Margalit's brilliant Concepts in Wine Technology is still one of the most widely used academic text books on the technology of winemaking in print. With exquisite detail, the book outlines every level of the vinification process, from the vineyard to the cellar. Paperback, 6 x 9 inches, 224pp, illustrated, index, appendixes.

$29.95. ISBN: 0-932664-66-0

A Wine-Growers' Guide

Philip M. Wagner

The best-selling "how to grow wine grapes" guide in print, this classic text has been the mainstay of both professional and dilettante vineyardists for more than a decade. The book includes information on propagating, planting, training and pruning vines; and vine ailments and vineyard management. Paperback, 5 ½ x 8 ½ inches, 240pp, illustrated.

$19.95. ISBN: 978-0-932664-92-1

WINE BOOK PUBLISHER OF THE YEAR
GOURMAND WORLD BOOK AWARDS, 2004

The Wine Appreciation Guild has been an educational pioneer in our fascinating community.
—Robert Mondavi

Your opinion matters to us…

You may not think it, but customer input is important to the ultimate quality of any revised work or second edition. We invite and appreciate any comments you may have. And by registering your WAG books you are enrolled to receive pre-publication discounts, special offers, or alerts to various wine events, only avail-able to registered members.

REGISTRATION FORM

Name_____Date_____

Professional Affiliation_____

Address_____

_____

City_____State_____Zip_____

e-mail_____

What book or other product did you purchase?_____

How did you discover this book (or other product)?_____

_____

Was this book required class reading? Y/N

School/Organiztion_____

Where did you acquire this book?_____

Was it a good read? (circle)	Poor	1	2	3	Excellent
Was it useful to your work? (circle)	Poor	1	2	3	Excellent

Suggestions_____

_____

_____

Comments_____

_____

_____

You can register your book by phone: (800) 231-9463; Fax: (650) 866-3513; e-mail: Info@WineAppreciation.com; or snail mail (copy and send to: Product Registration, Wine Appreciation Guild, 360 Swift Avenue, South San Francisco, CA 94080).